Woodland & Wildlife

Keith Kirby

WHITTET BOOKS

First published 1992
© 1992 by Keith Kirby
Whittet Books Ltd, 18 Anley Road, London W14 0BY
Illustrations and design by Richard Kelly

British Library Cataloguing in Publication Data

Kirby, Keith
 Woodland and wildlife.
 I. Title
 333.750941

ISBN 0 905483 96 0

Acknowledgments

I must acknowledge the efforts of many colleagues, friends
and previous workers, both inside and outside the Nature
Conservancy Council, whose ideas I have plundered for
this book. Please forgive the lack of references. All mistakes,
omissions, misinterpretations and totally crackpot ideas are
of course uniquely my own. Finally, this is a personal view
of woodland conservation and does not necessarily coincide
with that of the Nature Conservancy Council or of
English Nature.

Typeset by Litho Link Ltd, Welshpool, Powys, Wales
Printed and bound by WBC

Contents

Introduction

The clearance of the natural forests in Britain started thousands of years ago and only in the last century has the decline in our total woodland cover been reversed. Even so we have much less woodland than most of our European neighbours. As the European Community (EC) moves towards greater unity a Common Forestry Programme may emerge. Already the Irish Republic has made use of Community funds to expand its forest estate; Britain, with its generally favourable climate for tree growth, might also be seen as a priority area for forest expansion.

Would the resources allocated to British forestry and conservation be better used for forestry programmes overseas? We can and do help world forest conservation directly, through research and through aid to forestry, wildlife and national park programmes, but we should also lead by example.

In Britain we import tropical hardwoods from all the great rainforest areas of the world, yet very little of it comes from sustainable sources. The main clearance of tropical forest, involving the loss of many species and the displacement of indigenous peoples, is for farming and development schemes, but often the clearance follows the opening up of a region to loggers. Of course clearance may be followed by re-planting or regeneration and some timber firms argue that only by maintaining and controlling the timber trade can such forests gain a value that will prevent their total destruction. This is an attractive idea. It remains to be seen if it can be made to work on a large scale.

It is not only in the tropics that more wood is being cut than is being grown anew. The same is true in many of the great conifer forests that stretch across from Canada through Scandinavia and Russia. Logging in Russia may increase in the next few years to provide the exports and hence the hard currency needed to improve the standard of living of the Russian peoples. Britain, as one of the world's major timber importers, benefits from this trade, but should we ignore its effects on the environment of the exporting country? Should we increase the amount of home-grown timber to reduce the strain on forests elsewhere?

The burning of tropical forests, sometimes linked to projects funded by British banks or companies, contributes to the 'greenhouse effect' by releasing large amounts of carbon dioxide into the atmosphere. Planting new forests in Britain counteracts this in a very small way, but not if most of the wood is made into short-lived paper. Nor is it sensible for this purpose to plant forests on peat bogs as has been common practice in Britain, if one aim is to reduce the amount of carbon dioxide in the atmosphere. Such planting releases the carbon that has been stored, sometimes for thousands of years, in the bog itself.

WOODLAND COVER IN EUROPE

Ireland	5%	France	27%
The Netherlands	9%	Norway	27%
Great Britain	10%	Germany	30%
Denmark	12%	Spain	31%
Greece	20%	Portugal	40%
Belgium & Luxembourg	21%	Sweden	64%
Italy	22%	Finland	76%

Although we may not have so many woods as our European neighbours, ours offer a unique variety of plants and animals: they are home, for instance, to the Scottish crossbill, a distinct species found largely in the native pinewoods of Scotland; they contain ferns and mosses very rare in the rest of Europe; and they (together with Ireland) probably have more bluebells than in the whole of the rest of the world. Similarly our moors and bogs have exceptionally high populations of wading birds and raptors such as golden eagles as well as some ten per cent of all the blanket bogs in the world. What do we want to happen to these species and communities in the next decade?

For the last twelve years I have been fortunate to work, first, for the Nature Conservancy Council in Great Britain, and now for its successor, English Nature, looking at woods, trying to work out the best ways to conserve them and their wildlife. I hope this book will help you to understand the issues involved and make you feel that that is a worthwhile aim.

I hope that we can hand on to our children as rich a variety of woodland wildlife as we have received, because I believe we have a responsibility for the other species that inhabit this planet. This applies as much to the yellow-necked mouse in Britain as to the tiger in India. In addition to the aesthetic and spiritual reasons for conserving our wildlife, there are more utilitarian ones: wild plants and animals have proved to be sensitive indicators of different types of pollution – lichens disappeared from around many of our towns because the levels of sulphur dioxide were too high; streams without fish suggest serious acidification and high levels of dissolved aluminium which may not be good for our health; while the decline and subsequent recovery of the peregrine and sparrowhawk in Britain are related to the use and then banning of certain types of pesticide. Native pine woods may help to provide the answer to the pine beauty moth problem, which is a very damaging pest of lodgepole pine plantations in Scotland, but does not cause serious damage in its natural host, the Scots pine. Wild populations of birch, which is receiving much attention from foresters at present as a potential commercial timber tree, may supply the types that will be suitable for planting in new forests.

Insensitive forestry schemes can damage not only woodland but also plants and animals of open ground. There have been substantial losses of our most important wildlife over the last fifty years as a result of the spread of plantations designed largely according to simple commercial criteria. If forests and forest production are to be increased in Britain this must now be done in a way that maintains the wildlife surviving from the former natural forests of this country and does not destroy the wild moors and bogs that are the home for some of our most spectacular birds and unusual plant communities. This will cost money; here I will try to show the value of what we should be conserving in Britain; where our priorities should lie; where are the greatest opportunities but also where the greatest losses will be if we make the wrong decisions.

I

Every One is Different

Woods may seem unchanging because the life cycles of trees are so much longer than ours, but over the last 100 years there have been more alterations in our woodland cover and its composition than in the previous 2,000. Some of the myriad plants and animals that inhabit even the smallest wood have become more common as a result, others have declined massively or become extinct.

None of our woods now is exactly like the natural forest, the wildwood, that once covered much of Britain (see chapter 2), even though many of the species from the wildwood can be found in them. Good examples are the wood at Gaitbarrows in Lancashire which contains over 900 different types of fungi, Wytham Woods in Oxfordshire which has over 3,000 species of insects and other invertebrates, Ebernoe Common in Sussex and the woods along the River Findhorn south-east of Nairn which each have more than 300 ferns, grasses and flowers, while Ty-canol Wood in Pembrokeshire has over 100 species of mosses and liverworts and 170 species of lichen. Chapters 3-6 describe the origin and spread of different types of wood and the wildlife they are likely to contain. This indicates which areas are most important if we are to keep the last descendants of natural woodland, the habitats for rare plants and animals and those with the greatest variety of species. Very few woods will be kept just for nature conservation, however; so how to decide what other uses will be compatible with that aim?

Woodland uses

The major use of wood in much of our history was for fuel, as it still is for about half the world's population. Today many of the small trees cut in Britain go to make paper. One tree makes roughly 33,000 sheets of A4 paper and each of us uses about two trees' worth of paper products each year.

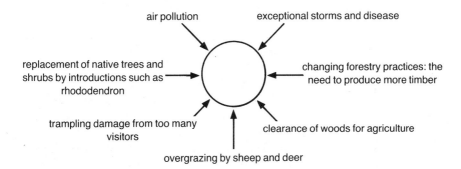

The pressures on a wood.

Wood is a marvellous material to work with. Neolithic wooden trackways more than 5,000 years old have been found in the peat bogs of Somerset and Cumbria. Massive wooden palisades whose remains have been traced at Mount Pleasant near Dorchester and Avebury (Wiltshire) required the cutting of thousands of metres of tree trunks. The actual remains of 3,000-year-old wooden buildings from the Bronze Age can be seen at the Flag Fen excavations near Peterborough standing on an artificial island constructed from two million pieces of wood. A Saxon nave at Greensted Church (Essex); further north the majestic twelfth-century barn at Coggeshall; the half of the ill-fated Mary Rose rescued from Portsmouth harbour and many later buildings and ships show what could be made and built without modern power tools.

If woods are to be valued not just for the production of timber, but for an intrinsic value as habitat for blackcaps and brimstones, daffodils and dormice, there will be a price to pay, whether it is reducing timber production, controlling grazing or recreation or altering the course of a road.

Types of woodland

Some woods are older than our oldest cathedrals. Such woods have an almost infinite variety in terms of types of tree, and how they are growing, which depends in part on the way soils and climate have shaped them, though for at least the last 5,000 years, the axes of our ancestors have been as important an influence.

To take just a small part of one particular area: Witherslack Edge in the south of the Lake District. Immediately below the Edge are some of the finest woods in Britain, mixtures of oak, ash, hazel, elm and small-leaved lime, trees that have been common in these woods for thousands of years. They contain primroses, anemones, daffodils and a host of other wild flowers, insects and birds. However, few of the trees are more than one hundred years old, most are much less, for the wood has been cut many times in its long history. Consequently some trees grow not with a single stem, but as a cluster of small 'poles', all coming from a gnarled old stump. Scattered old pines and some massive cherries were probably planted in the nineteenth century. Thus the age and type of tree and how they have grown indicate how the woods have been treated in the past.

Nearby, small regularly shaped blocks were planted perhaps to improve the appearance of the fields around Witherslack Hall. The pine on Farrers Allotment and the dark mass of spruce on Foulshaw Moss were established to meet our present need for coniferous timber. The young birches growing in patches on the edge of the plateau grassland have managed to grow away despite the nibbling of sheep, perhaps during a period when the numbers of animals on the top were fewer than now.

This area provides a starting point for looking at how woods in Britain as a whole may be classified and described, which in turn helps to explain the plants and animals that may be found in them. The woods below the Edge are described as **ancient** not because they contain many very big old trees

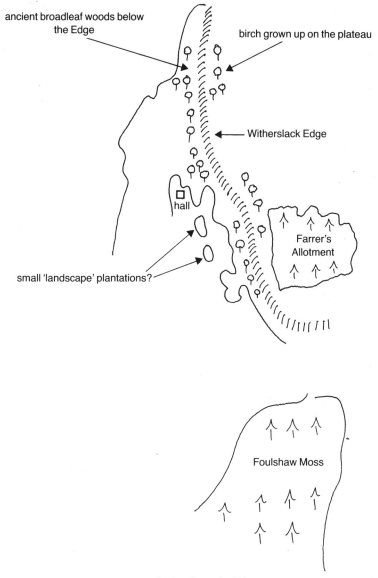

ancient broadleaf woods below the Edge

birch grown up on the plateau

Witherslack Edge

hall

Farrer's Allotment

small 'landscape' plantations?

Foulshaw Moss

A view from the Edge.

(although they may) but because the ground has almost certainly been wooded since medieval times and probably for very much longer. Some ancient woods are the direct descendants of the wildwood, the natural forest that once covered Britain. Ancient woods are contrasted with the woods that have grown up or been planted from the seventeenth century onward on land that was formerly grassland, moor, arable or some other open ground (like the blocks around Witherslack Hall). These latter are called **recent** woods. Ancient woods (described in chapters 3, 4) are usually more varied and contain more rare and interesting species than do recent woods (chapters 5, 6), given that both have received similar treatment.

Within both the ancient and recent woods a difference can be seen between the woods where the trees have been deliberately planted, **plantations** (chapters 4, 6), and those areas composed of trees grown from seeds or stump regrowth, which are called **semi-natural** 'stands', or groups of trees (chapters 3, 5). 'Semi-natural' is a somewhat clumsy phrase, but one that is widely used to indicate that both people and the natural environment have shaped a particular piece of wood, with the latter being at least as important as the former. Semi-natural stands are generally more varied in their composition and structure and hence more important for nature conservation than plantations. In the latter there is likely to be much more emphasis placed on the production of timber.

The trees and shrubs can be split into two broad groups, one of which is described as **broadleaved** and includes oak, ash, lime, hazel and holly, while the other, including spruce, pine and juniper, is **coniferous**. There are perhaps 1,700 species of tree growing in Britain, if those in botanic gardens and parks are included, but less than 100 are **native**, that is they have spread to and through Britain by themselves, without human intervention. Most of Britain lies within the broad climatic zone that stretches across Europe where broadleaved trees predominate in the natural forests. We have just three native conifers – Scots pine, yew and juniper. Of these only the Scots pine survives in extensive semi-natural stands, in woods in the central and north Highlands; yew and juniper are scattered through the country usually as small groves, as they are in the woods of the Witherslack area.

Throughout Britain, however, trees have been planted in woods and areas where they are not native. Scots pine is now common in southern England and beech grows in Scotland, while many others have been brought from overseas. These **introductions** include the spruces so favoured by modern forestry, which now make up more than a third of the country's forests. Introduced shrubs such as rhododendron and snowberry have been widely planted to provide more cover for that introduced bird, the pheasant. Fallow deer brought in by the Romans and muntjac (a more recent import from the Far East) chew their way through the undergrowth, particularly in southern England. The grey squirrel from North America runs riot in the woods of England and Wales and is spreading in Scotland.

Introduced species are not all bad: they can be attractive and useful. Some have been here so long that they form part of traditional landscapes. Sycamore was introduced to Britain from the mountains of continental Europe probably in the Middle Ages, but now where would the Pennine farmhouse be without its sheltering sycamore? Sweet chestnut, thought to have been brought over by the Romans, has been abundant in the south-east for so long that it is sometimes regarded as an honorary native in parts of Kent. However in most woods introduced species compete with and replace our native species; they disrupt the patterns established over hundreds or thousands of years, and may limit the habitat for indigenous wildlife, so that there are times and places where introduced species need to be controlled.

Overall the most important woods for nature conservation are those that have existed for longest, the ancient woods, because they may be descended from the wild wood; those that are composed of native species rather than introductions; and those that have grown up naturally rather than being created as plantations. Yet it is a curious fact that most British woodland is planted, most is composed of introduced conifers and most did not exist a hundred years ago.

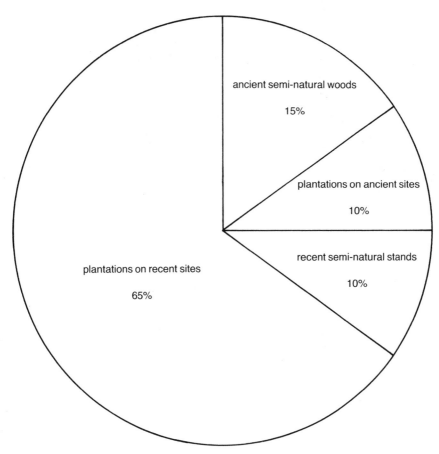

A breakdown of British woodland by origin and current composition.

THE ORIGIN AND COMPOSITION OF BRITISH WOODS

% OF FOREST AREA OCCUPIED BY:

Sitka spruce	28	*Introduced from North America*
Scots pine	13	*(mainly outside its native range)*
Oaks	9	

Larches	8	*Introduced from the Continent and Japan*
Lodgepole pine	7	*Introduced from North America*
Norway spruce	6	*Introduced from the Continent*
Ash	4	
Beech	4	
Birches	4	
Corsican pine	2	*Introduced from southern Europe*
Douglas fir	2	*Introduced from North America*

EXTENT OF WOODLAND IN BRITAIN

ENGLAND	% LAND SURFACE (ALL WOODLAND)	% LAND SURFACE (ANCIENT WOODLAND ONLY)
Avon	5.1	2.4
Beds	5.0	2.1
Berks	5.5	4.6
Bucks	8.3	4.5
Cambs	1.9	0.8
Cheshire	3.8	0.7
Cleveland	5.7	2.5
Cornwall	5.1	1.9
Cumbria	8.0	2.3
Derby	5.0	1.7
Devon	8.0	2.2
Dorset	9.4	2.9
Durham	5.7	1.7
East Sussex	15.6	10.4
Essex	4.1	2.4
Glos	10.0	6.7
Hants	16.4	6.8
Hereford	8.2	5.7

Herts	7.6	3.3
Humberside	2.7	0.2
Isle of Wight	9.7	4.1
Kent	11.4	8.0
Lancs	3.7	1.0
Leics	3.0	1.0
Lincs	3.2	1.0
London (GLC)	3.8	1.6
Manchester (GMC)	2.0	0.6
Merseyside	2.6	0.2
Norfolk	7.9	0.5
Northants	5.0	2.7
Northumberland	15.2	1.0
N. Yorks	6.7	1.7
Notts	6.9	1.0
Oxon	5.9	2.8
Salop	7.2	2.7
S. Yorks	6.7	2.8
Somerset	5.6	2.6
Staffs	6.2	2.1
Suffolk	7.4	1.1
Surrey	18.8	5.8
Tyne & Wear	3.1	2.0
Warwicks	3.5	2.1
W. Midlands	2.0	0.8
W. Yorks	4.6	1.7
W. Sussex	17.3	8.5
Wilts	7.1	3.6
Worcs	6.5	3.5

WALES

Clwyd	9.1	2.2
Dyfed	10.4	2.3
Glamorgan	15.3	3.0
Gwent	12.3	6.4
Gwynedd	11.0	1.7
Powys	12.7	3.1

SCOTLAND (Regions)

Borders	15.8	0.4
Central	13.7	2.3
Dumfries & Galloway	22.2	1.2
Fife	9.4	0.3
Grampian	15.1	1.3
Highland	9.6	2.7
Lothian	8.2	1.3
Strathclyde	15.2	2.2
Tayside	9.4	1.2

Woodland change over the last 100-150 years

The amount of woodland in Britain has gone through periods of decline and most recently of expansion. The speed of these changes is very apparent when modern maps are compared with those produced in the early to mid-nineteenth century. Such maps include the early editions of the Ordnance Survey which are often available in local libraries.

The changes that have occurred vary from place to place. The Thetford area in Norfolk had very little woodland in the early nineteenth century, but is now a mass of trees, mainly pine, planted on the shifting sands of the Breck in the '20s and '30s. The woods in north Buckinghamshire have remained much the same size or been slightly reduced through clearance for farming or mineral working, but many areas that were broadleaved are now coniferous or mixtures of broadleaves and conifers. Argyll was comparatively well wooded along the valley sides, and many of these broadleaved sites remain, but there has been much expansion of new planting, and again a replacement of old oak woods by

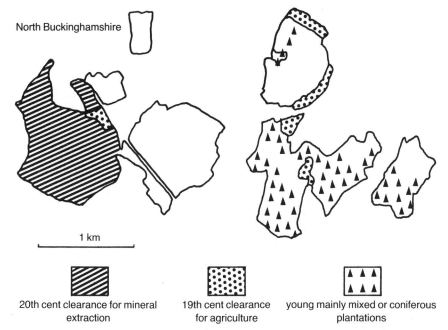

North Buckinghamshire

1 km

20th cent clearance for mineral
extraction

19th cent clearance
for agriculture

young mainly mixed or coniferous
plantations

In this part of Buckinghamshire there has been substantial loss of woodland (mainly to a quarry) and conversion of broadleaves to conifers.

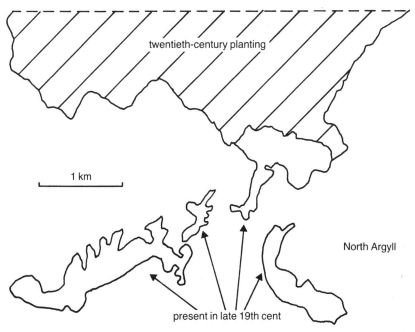

twentieth-century planting

1 km

North Argyll

present in late 19th cent

In this part of Argyll woods present in the nineteenth century have survived much as before, but there has been a very great increase due to new twentieth-century planting.

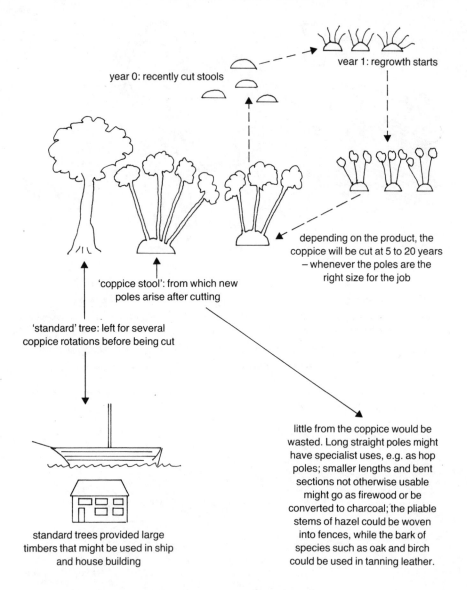

year 0: recently cut stools

year 1: regrowth starts

depending on the product, the coppice will be cut at 5 to 20 years – whenever the poles are the right size for the job

'coppice stool': from which new poles arise after cutting

'standard' tree: left for several coppice rotations before being cut

little from the coppice would be wasted. Long straight poles might have specialist uses, e.g. as hop poles; smaller lengths and bent sections not otherwise usable might go as firewood or be converted to charcoal; the pliable stems of hazel could be woven into fences, while the bark of species such as oak and birch could be used in tanning leather.

standard trees provided large timbers that might be used in ship and house building

The coppice cycle and its products.

conifers. Results from a series of regional studies have been put together to form a view of the overall change that has taken place.

Many woods that existed in the early nineteenth century are no longer there. In most cases they have been cleared to provide more farmland, but some have gone to make way for new roads, towns and quarries. These account for a loss of about 8 per cent of ancient woodland in England and Wales over the last 50 years and the losses in Scotland have been of a similar order.

Elsewhere much new woodland has come into existence. In the uplands of north and west Britain this has largely been through planting on a very big scale, but such plantations also exist in the lowlands, sometimes on old heaths as in Dorset or on dunes as at Newborough Warren (Anglesey). Many new small bits of woodland have been planted, particularly recently, on farms, along motorways and trunk roads. Woodland has also spread naturally on the downs and on Surrey commons and in parts of the Highlands following reductions in grazing and burning, and the drying out of bogs and fens.

Overall the total area of woodland has doubled from about 4-5 per cent at the turn of the century to about 10 per cent of the country now. However for wildlife the change in the distribution and composition of the woods is as important as the change in the total area.

A hundred years ago many woods were managed by **coppicing**. The trees were cut down to a stump, from which would spring a series of poles; after five to twenty years, according to the size of pole wanted, the poles could be cut and the process repeated more or less indefinitely. The Bradfield Woods in Suffolk, for example, appear to have been cut down (coppiced) 70 times in the last 700 years, but far from destroying the woods this probably ensured their survival since what the coppice produced was an important part of the rural economy.

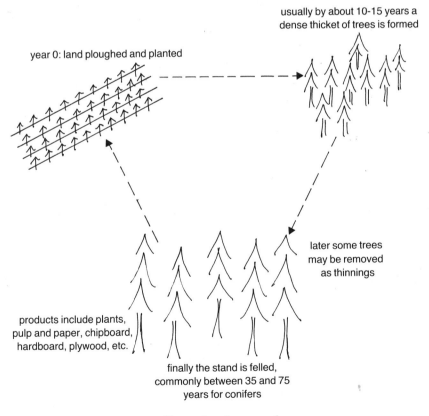

usually by about 10-15 years a dense thicket of trees is formed

year 0: land ploughed and planted

later some trees may be removed as thinnings

products include plants, pulp and paper, chipboard, hardboard, plywood, etc.

finally the stand is felled, commonly between 35 and 75 years for conifers

The modern forestry cycle.

In parts of Kent the commonest tree to find in coppice was sweet chestnut and its poles were used in the hop fields. In Hampshire and Dorset there were acres and acres of hazel cut to make the spars that held the thatch on to roofs and were woven into fencing hurdles – vast numbers of such hurdles were needed by the shepherds grazing sheep on the downs. In parts of Wales, northern England and Scotland the coppices were mainly of oak and were cut in the spring so that the bark could be stripped easily from the poles to produce tannin. Other trees also had special uses – alder and alder buckthorn were particularly valued for making gunpowder charcoal – but much of the wood was simply used as fuel.

When the coppice was cut regularly most of the trees were small. A scatter of larger trees known as **standards** might be left. These would be cut when they were larger, perhaps 70-80 years old, to be used in building or other jobs that required bigger timbers. Because different sections of the wood were cut in each year the woods tended to be light and airy; there were many open glades and newly cut patches.

COPPICING AND COPPICE PRODUCTS

Alder	*turnery (brush heads, chair legs)*
Ash	*turnery, thatching sways, scythe and tool handles, split rails*
Birch	*turnery, horse jumps*
Hazel	*bean and pea sticks, thatching spars, wattle fencing*
Hornbeam	*firewood*
Lime	*turnery*
Oak	*fencing (round, cleft or sawn)*
Sweet chestnut	*fencing*

Modern forestry works to a different pattern. Most wood goes for pulp and paper-making or is converted into chipboard, hardboard and plywood. Long straight planks are favoured by the construction and furniture trades. The need is therefore for a high volume of uniform material which can be produced more easily from conifers, which grow faster than most of our native broadleaves on comparable sites. For conifers in Britain the **rotation** (the time from planting to felling) is about 35–70 years, while for beech and oak 100 and 120 years are more common. The trees are harvested using tractors and specialized machinery and, as in most businesses, the larger the area treated at one time the more economical is the whole process.

The character of British woodland has altered over the last century because of these changes in the pattern of forestry and the demands for wood products.

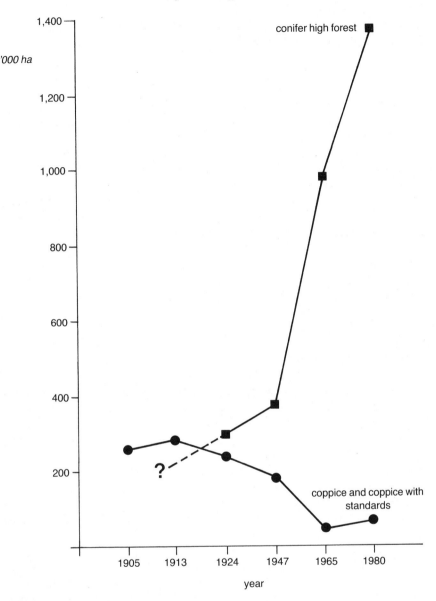

The rise of conifers and decline of coppice.

More conifers than broadleaves have been planted, even in woods that a hundred years ago were entirely broadleaved; very few woods are still coppiced; many small woods are neglected because modern methods of working are more suited to large-scale forestry. Such neglected woods are much darker and more shaded than they were when they were regularly cut.

In many places, though, the woods have changed less than the surrounding countryside, which has been transformed as a result of technological developments in farming and the policies to increase food production adopted by successive governments from 1945 until the early 1980s.

Changes on the farm

About 80 per cent of the ancient woods that have been cleared completely in the last fifty years have been replaced by farming. Hedgerows that once linked woods and provided corridors for the spread of plants and animals from one wood to another have been grubbed out to make bigger fields. Many woodland insects need nectar from flowers in their adult stage. Once they would have found these in herb-rich hay-meadows and green-lanes next to the woods. Probably more than 90 per cent of such lowland meadows have now gone, ploughed and reseeded, sprayed or treated with high levels of nitrogen fertilizers to increase the yield of grass at the expense of their species richness.

The role of woods as havens for wildlife on lowland farms has increased as other semi-natural areas on the farm have disappeared. Flowery rides and glades within the wood must now provide a substitute for these habitats. However the increasing isolation of each wood among hectares of corn or improved grassland makes that wildlife more vulnerable to adverse natural or man-induced changes.

Upland farms and landscapes have also altered. Moorland has been 'improved' by ploughing and fertilizer treatment; other areas are grazed more heavily or burnt more regularly than in the past. Heather has given way to rough grassland which supports lower numbers of birds and insects. Few of the great expanses of bog in the north and west remain as they were: cutting for peat, once purely for domestic heating, has become a major industry; many other bogs have been drained and planted. Upland oakwoods are often so over-grazed by sheep and deer that there is little or no regeneration. The walls that once kept these animals out while the young trees needed protection have fallen into disrepair.

There are now moves to try and restore or rejuvenate these features of the countryside that are so important for wildlife. New hedges are being planted and old ones cut again; ponds are being dug and old ones cleared out; grants are available to help farmers fence woods against stock. Fields left fallow, under schemes within the EC to set aside land from agriculture, provide a new supply of seeds and insects as food for common farmland birds. However it will be some years before such initiatives start to have a significant effect on the wildlife of the countryside as a whole.

Many woods were once centres of industry, integrated with the rest of the local community. Farm labourers might switch to woodland work in the winter. After World War II the reduction in the numbers of people working on farms and the lack of much of an income from farm woods meant that they were generally neglected. Even where the woods are still managed the work is increasingly mechanized so that fewer people are needed. Major jobs may be put out to contractors who draw their work-force from nearby towns.

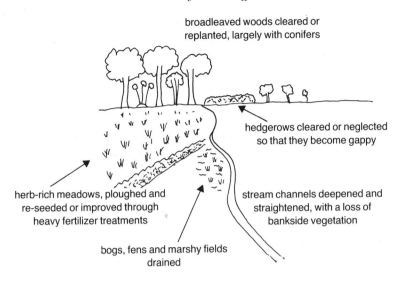

broadleaved woods cleared or
replanted, largely with conifers

hedgerows cleared or neglected
so that they become gappy

herb-rich meadows, ploughed and
re-seeded or improved through
heavy fertilizer treatments

stream channels deepened and
straightened, with a loss of
bankside vegetation

bogs, fens and marshy fields
drained

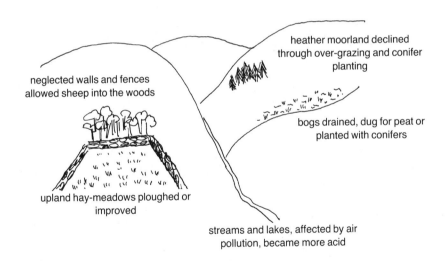

heather moorland declined
through over-grazing and conifer
planting

neglected walls and fences
allowed sheep into the woods

bogs drained, dug for peat or
planted with conifers

upland hay-meadows ploughed or
improved

streams and lakes, affected by air
pollution, became more acid

Landscapes under siege 1945-1980.

Fewer people work in the woods, but an increasing number are concerned about the appearance of the countryside and want to visit it in their spare time. My hunter-gatherer instincts reappear each autumn as the blackberries start to ripen. A more organized form of hunting – for pheasants – developed to such an extent during the last century that it is a major use of woods in lowland Britain today. Other people just want to go for a walk, using the paths our ancestors trod to get to and from work in the fields. There are also new distinctive twentieth-century pastimes such as rallying or orienteering in woods, which can seem at odds with the tranquillity we associate with woods.

Somehow, among all these changes, much of our woodland wildlife has survived, but often only just. The violet click beetle lives mainly in a few trees in Windsor Forest (although another site has just been found); the lady's slipper orchid is found just in one wood; populations of our largest gamebird, the capercaillie, are at a low ebb. We cannot rely on these species and even the abundance of common plants and animals surviving into the future without active help.

Fortunately there has been a dramatic increase in interest in nature conservation over the last twenty years. The interests of wildlife, wood production and other woodland uses can be integrated on most sites. Ever since people started to clear the wildwood, the woodland plants and animals have had to adapt to the changing conditions that we and our ancestors have imposed. Just how much conditions have changed we can try to assess by looking at what the wildwood was like.

2

Wildwood that is no More

Britain's climate has changed many times, having been both much colder, and much warmer than now. The plants and animals have changed also: where red deer now graze there have been musk oxen such as are found in Greenland, and at other times hippopotamus.

About 5,000–7,000 years ago, however, the climate was much as today, but, were you transported back, it would be difficult to recognize your local neighbourhood because it is covered by natural forests – the wildwood. Majestic oaks, limes and elms, more locally pines, shoot up 20-30 metres, others lie rotting at your feet. The root plates of the fallen trees stand 2-3 metres high. Gradually they will collapse to leave a mound of soil. In the hole from which the roots have been torn, water has collected and mosquitoes breed in abundance. Wild ox and boar drink from it. Red deer move through the undergrowth, carefully skirting round the tangle of a fallen tree's crown. Nearby a wolf howls.

If you are in the south of Britain the main tree about you is probably small-leaved lime. In the south-east hornbeam may form an understorey below the taller growing limes. Beech is present on free-draining soils. Oak is mainly as scattered old trees. In the west, lime is less prevalent, elm and ash take over where the soils are rich enough, with oak a much more equal partner in the canopy. Moving north, lime disappears altogether beyond what are now

Cumbria and Durham. In the Highlands pine starts to become common and dominates forests particularly in the east. Oak, ash and elm remain up the west coast, but become increasingly confined to the lower ground. Birch and hazel then take over. There are no sharp divisions between areas where one or another tree dominates. There are many gaps, but the overwhelming impression is of a landscape in which trees rule. Where did this wildwood come from and where did it go?

Putting together the pieces

The story of our present-day woods starts with the last ice age some 18,000 years ago. Not all of the country was covered by the glaciers but there were no continuous stretches of forest, although some trees may have survived in sheltered corners such as Islay. As the climate improved and the ice retreated so plants and animals spread back from south and west Europe. Recolonization was not a steady, straightforward affair. Mountain ranges and then, about 7,000 years ago, the Channel got in the way and slowed the spread of some species that were (and are) quite capable of growing in Britain. This is one reason why our woods differ from those of continental Europe, why they are special.

Much of what we know about the plants that covered Britain in the past comes from peat bogs and mud at the bottom of lakes. Each year plants produce vast amounts of pollen, only a small proportion of which ever reaches its intended destination, the female flowers. Much drifts in the air until it settles or is washed out by rain. Some of it lands in lakes or ponds, in peat bogs or in some types of acid soil, where a few of the thousands of grains may be preserved because the outer skin of the pollen grain is made of a substance which is very resistant to decay. Different species of plants have distinctive patterns on this outer skin so they can be recognized under the microscope.

As the peat in a bog or mud at the lake bottom builds up, each layer retains a proportion of the most recent additions of pollen. Differences between the pollen found in successive levels (the deeper the layer, the older it is) reflect changes in the abundance of different plants in the surrounding land. Pollen remains from all over Britain have been studied in this way. They help us to understand what was growing at a particular time and place, which in turn suggests what was happening to the climate and perhaps how our ancestors were living. Samples from the upper, more recent levels have higher proportions of pollen from species commonly found in arable fields and grassland and less from trees and shrubs. Thus there is a record of how the original forest, the wildwood, came to be cleared.

There may be other signs that the landscape was changing. Soil erosion often increases when hillsides are cleared of trees. A sudden increase in the annual build up of mud at the bottom of a lake may indicate that forests were being cut on the surrounding slopes. Traces of charcoal in the peat or mud may have come from natural fires, but were probably more often started by humans. Most dramatic of all are the large pieces of trunk or stumps, 'bog oaks' (actually often pine), that can sometimes be found in peat. Why were they not replaced when they died with younger trees? Was there a catastrophe or just a creeping change that caused the deaths of these trees? The answer sometimes lies in natural variations in the climate. Wetter conditions may have favoured the growth of bogs and stopped new trees growing. As the old trees died their remains were preserved. However, cutting and burning of the forest by our ancestors and grazing by their flocks could have helped to impoverish the soil, which might have accelerated the process of bog formation.

It is less easy to find out about the animals that were living in the forests of the past, but the rubbish dumps left around early settlements provide some clues. The bones of the mammals, birds and fishes used by the inhabitants as food, tools or company can be found and identified. Even the wing cases of beetles may be preserved in the mud at the bottom of ditches where lack of oxygen slows down their decomposition. Such finds are particularly valuable, because we can use the present-day habitats and food of the species as a guide to the conditions that must have prevailed when they fell into the ditch. If the beetles are now found only in areas much to the north of the site then it suggests that conditions were much colder then than now. If they are forest-dwellers then there must have been an abundance of trees even if now they are scarce.

As societies developed, we can find direct records of animals and plants, even descriptions of the forest itself, although by then the wildwood had probably already disappeared. Wolf and bear feature in Roman writings about Britain; Gerald of Monmouth tells us that the beaver in Wales in 1188 was only found in the River Teifi. Not that all such drawings and writings should be believed, however, or were there really dragons?

Long after these animals and even the forest had gone, an echo of them lived on in place names. In Cumbria there are, for example, 'Barbon' named from the old Norse for beaver (*bjorr*), 'Uldale', 'Ullock' and 'Ulpha' amongst others taken from the old Norse for wolf (*ulfr*) while the lime tree seems to have been much more common, to judge from the frequency of 'lind' names – 'Linbeck', 'Lincrag', 'Lindal', 'Lindale'. Names are ambiguous, however, even if their origin is clear – for instance, was Birchtree Hill so named because there were lots of birches there or because there was only one and its rarity made it memorable?

Finally in our quest for the lost wildwood of Britain we can look at undisturbed forests in North America and continental Europe and see how they behave. The major lesson to be learned from such studies is that there is no standard pattern for natural forests; they differ one from another and from place to place within them. Thus we must not expect the descendants of the wildwood to follow a single simple pattern.

It gets warmer

Pine, birch and hazel were the main trees in the first forests that formed after the last ice age as Britain got warmer. Later arrivals included alder, oak, elm and lime. Trees and shrubs whose seeds can be blown by the wind, such as

10,000 BC	8,000 BC	6,000 BC	4,000 BC	2,000 BC
			Neolithic period	
			Mesolithic period	
gradual spread of vegetation after retreat of the glaciers	birch, pine and hazel as the main forest species	ash, elm, oak and lime arrive and start to spread, displacing pine and birch	mixed forests probably reach their greatest extent. Beech starts to spread	major clearance of forest starts
			English Channel	
			5,500 BC	

Arrival and spread of trees in southern Britain.

birch and pine, may have spread very quickly once climate and soils became suitable. The heavier seeds of oak could have been carried by birds like jays who bury some as future food stores but do not recover them all. A population of trees under favourable conditions can 'migrate' in these ways at a rate of about 100-1,000 metres a year, so it would not take long for most of the country to be covered once the climate was suitable. Among the last species to arrive naturally were beech and hornbeam, and they did not spread much beyond the south and south-east.

The first colonists were spreading through a largely treeless landscape, but later arrivals had not only to get here but to compete with the ones that had come before. Initially, for example, pine and birch seedlings would fill the gaps in a pine-birch wood. However, once conditions were right for oak and it was in the region, oak regeneration would increasingly appear in the gaps. Shifts in the composition of a piece of woodland would have been gradual. For a long time, pine might still be present as large old trees. Later when small-leaved lime arrived most of the seedlings would have tended to be of this species, since it can stand more shade and grow in smaller gaps than can oak. Then in turn the oak would have become restricted to a scatter of very old trees.

Not that any tree species was lost altogether from Britain in the process as far as we know. Pine which could thrive in cold conditions remained common in the north and high in the mountains. It was probably also found in small pockets of particularly acid, peaty or sandy soils. Woods where hazel formed the main canopy may have been pushed to the north-west of Scotland, where they still occur, but it could grow well as an understorey species in the rest of Britain and is still one of the commonest woodland shrubs. Birch remained a major tree in the Highlands but elsewhere may have led a fugitive existence, coming in when

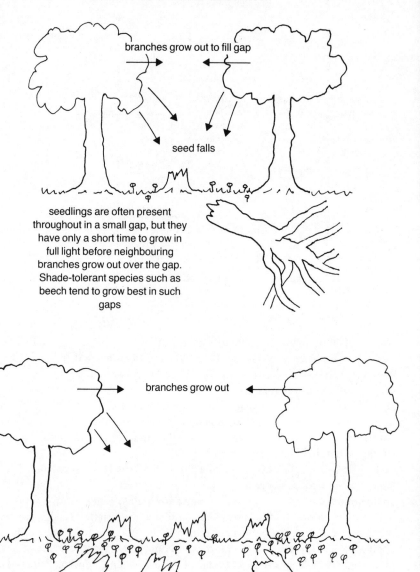

branches grow out to fill gap

seed falls

seedlings are often present throughout in a small gap, but they have only a short time to grow in full light before neighbouring branches grow out over the gap. Shade-tolerant species such as beech tend to grow best in such gaps

branches grow out

in large gaps seedlings may be densest round the edge. For several years there may be few seedlings in the centre of the gap which is furthest from the parent tree. In the centre of large gaps species like oak or birch may find enough light to grow and thrive.

Gaps in the forest.

large gaps appeared or at the forest edges where there was plenty of light. And even when conditions for trees were most favourable, there would always have been gaps in the forest.

Openings in the forest

Forests once grew on Shetland and Orkney which are now largely treeless, and there were only a few places such as the peat bogs of northern Scotland that have never had a full woodland cover for more than very short periods. The pine stumps that can be found in them come from a brief spell some 3,000 years ago when it was dry enough for the trees to grow on the peat; since then it has always been too wet. The tops of some mountains over about 650m were, and still are, also beyond the natural tree line. On the coast, wind and salt-spray may have kept cliff tops clear of trees, while there were extensive low lying areas of fen swamp in some valleys. Overall, however, perhaps 80 per cent of the country was wooded.

In this forest gaps would have formed when trees fell or were blown over, as happened on a grand scale in 1968 in Scotland or in 1987 in southern England. Trees are frequently struck by lightning and in the pine forests of the north this could have led to large-scale natural fires. Broadleaved forests further south in Britain would not have burned easily. Mature trees are unlikely to be killed by light grass or bracken fires, but on the rare occasions when fierce fires did occur, quite large open areas may have been created.

Other trees would have been killed by fungi, or died after their leaves had been stripped by insects. Beavers cut trees for food along streams and rivers, while promising patches of regeneration might be stripped of their bark and killed by deer which use them as fraying posts. So a series of smaller gaps would have been produced, some of which might have remained open for several years. Fungus surviving in dead stumps and decaying roots for example might have killed nearby saplings, perhaps a thriving bracken bed developed which smothered any seedlings, or they might have been eaten by the grazing animals that roamed the forests, the wild ox, red and roe deer. Other gaps would have been temporary, rapidly filled with young trees and shrubs or by the spread of branches from trees on the edge.

The wildwood was no uniform blanket, but a shifting mosaic of trees of different ages and species. Suddenly a single big tree would have collapsed as centuries of root rot finally took their toll. The small gap would have created opportunities for seedlings from the surrounding trees, but only if they could grow in partial shade, as can beech or lime. Often the gap in the canopy closed through branches from neighbouring trees growing in from the edge, before the sapling had a chance to reach the canopy. It had to wait for another gap to occur before resuming its race to the sky. Elsewhere a much larger gap formed after a major storm; more light and better growing conditions ensured that a wider range of trees could get established. The centre of a gap may have taken longer to fill, because it was further from the trees on the gap edge, and so an uneven aged mixture of young trees developed. Such large gaps allowed light-

north-west: high rainfall, more high altitude areas, older rocks, more acidic soils and peats

central and eastern Highlands: links to Scandinavian climate. Cold winters.

(melancholy thistle, Scots pine, downy birch, twinflower, globeflower)

declining temperatures to the north

links to continental climate

(hornbeam, beech, small leaved lime, yellow archangel, pedunculate oak)

western seaboard: influenced by Atlantic Gulf Stream giving relatively mild winters and very wet conditions.

(holly, madder, climbing fumitory, hay-scented fern, bog myrtle)

'uplands'

'uplands

'lowlands'

'uplands'

south-east: generally low rainfall, high summer temperatures, low altitude, high proportion of base rich soils, little peat

links to southern continental climate

(clematis, spurge laurel, field maple, butcher's broom, large leaved lime)

Patterns in environment.

demanding trees like ash and oak to regenerate in a beech or lime forest, or birch to spread in oak and pine woods, even though over the forest as a whole the reverse changes were more common. Trees grow at different rates so the frequency with which gaps occurred in the forest would have varied according to the main species present.

Natural gaps and glades were probably the original habitats for plants and animals, such as butterflies, that are associated now with the first few years after an area has been felled. Some of the species of grassland and lowland heath were perhaps once found mainly in woodland glades and may still turn up there. The common plantain and weeds of disturbed ground may have been quite rare until the forests started to be cleared.

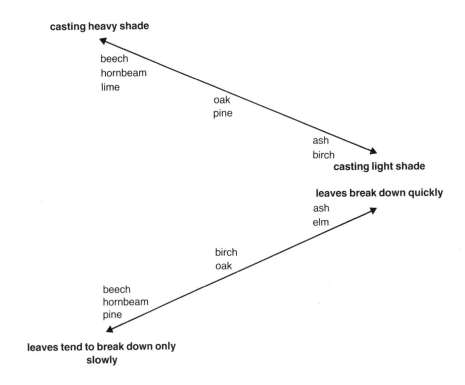

Variations on variations: diversity in the wildwood

Regional variation in the wildwood was probably very high: for instance, the rainfall in Essex is about 50 cm a year, while in the heart of the Lake District it may be more than 200 cm. The south-east has a wide mixture of often very fertile soils (that is why it has the most arable land) while the rocks of the north-west give rise to generally acid, poor soils. These differences in climate and geology would have been reflected in the composition of the wildwood, just as their effects are still visible in the ancient semi-natural woods that are its descendants (see the next chapter). Broad-scale regional variations would have been created, within which smaller-scale differences in soils and topography would elaborate the pattern further.

Differences in the make-up of the tree and shrub layer have a profound effect on everything else in a forest. If you compare ash and beech growing on the same site you will usually find much more of a cover of flowers and brambles under the ash than the beech, which will usually have a dense surface layer of litter. Hoverflies looking for nectar are much more likely to feed in the ash area but spiders that hunt among litter will be more common under the beech.

Insects and other invertebrates similarly exploit the various parts of trees in different ways. Amongst those that live on leaves, some caterpillars feed directly on the leaf surface, others roll the leaf up and feed in the protective tube formed, yet others live actually inside the leaf, excavating meandering mines through the green tissue. Aphids and plant bugs such as leaf hoppers feed by piercing the surface of the leaves, while gall wasps stimulate the plant to produce a mass of extra tissue that grows round and enfolds the grub to give the familiar oak apple, spangle and marble galls. Perhaps in response to such attacks, some trees such as oaks develop large amounts of tannin in their leaves, which makes them less palatable – at least when the leaves are old. This also slows the breakdown of the leaves on the ground. By contrast, the soft leaves of ash, which are attacked by fewer types of insect when they are on the tree, lack such compounds and are rapidly decomposed once they fall.

Other species attack the bark and wood. In one particular group of four beetles that live on ash, one feeds mainly in the thick bark of the trunk, two others prefer fallen trunks and boughs, but one goes for larger pieces, the other for small, and the last of the quartet bores into twigs. Thus the food resource has come to be shared out with relatively little overlap between potentially competing species.

The structure of the bark can be important. An old oak provides many more fissures and crevices in which insects, woodlice or snails can hide than does beech, with its smooth bark, or even a young oak. In turn this may mean that it is more worthwhile for a tree creeper to spend time searching for food on such old oaks.

In the gap formed where a tree or group of trees died there may be enough light for violets to spread and flower profusely and for plants more typical of open ground such as the marsh thistle to appear. Perhaps by the second year conditions will be suitable for fritillary butterflies to lay their eggs on the violets, while the thistle flowers provide food for the adults. Deer crop the tall herbs and grasses that develop in the following years of the gap. But if regeneration is successful, and young trees grow to form a thicket, many of these herbs become shaded out as a dense thicket develops. The violets survive in the shade but hardly flower; they are no longer suitable as food plants for the butterflies. Deer now use the area to lie up in, but find little food. On the other hand the dense low cover is good for nesting warblers such as whitethroat.

Different species of tree support varying numbers and species of insects; some regularly have more types of lichen on their bark than others; they fruit at different seasons providing a diverse though sometimes uncertain banquet for birds and small mammals.

However even where a block of the wildwood was composed mainly of one species there would have been a considerable variety of conditions and hence of wildlife over time. Birds nest and feed at different places on a single tree. The plants and animals that multiply in the gap formed by the death of a tree are gradually replaced by a different set as young trees form a dense, fairly shady

NUMBERS OF PLANT-EATING INSECTS AND MITES
ASSOCIATED WITH FOREST TREES IN BRITAIN
(based on the list compiled by Kennedy and Southwood in 1984)

Sallow and willows	450	Ash	68
Oak	423	Rowan	58
Birch	334	Lime	57
Poplar and aspen	189	Hornbeam	51
Scots pine	172	Maple	51
Alder	141	Juniper	32
Elm	124	Sweet chestnut	11
Crab apple	118	Holly	10
Hazel	106	Yew	6
Beech	98		

thicket. As the trees grow, some die naturally as the more vigorous overtop and then shade out their contemporaries. Gradually enough light gets through gaps in the canopy for plants on the woodland floor and in the shrub layer to flourish again.

These cyclical changes in the ground flora and birds can be seen easily in modern woods, but there is another set of players who are not so obvious. Indeed in most woods now they are severely depleted, but their role in natural forests cannot be overstated. They are the hidden army of species, particularly fungi, flies, beetles and bacteria that break down wood, leaf litter and dead animals and allow their nutrients to be recycled.

In the wildwood where trees were not harvested the heartwood of many standing trees would probably have been rotted away to leave a hollow shell of living tissue. The heartwood is not essential for the tree to survive and its removal by rotting fungi might even be advantageous: the nutrients in it are put back into circulation and the hollow cylindrical trunk left may be more flexible, and so better able to withstand high winds than a solid trunk.

Much of the wildlife of the wildwood probably depended on the habitats provided by these forest veterans. Apart from wood-rotting insects and fungi there are at least ten species of bat that roost, breed or hibernate in hollow trees and about a third of the birds that regularly breed in a wood use many holes or dead wood in some form or other.

Once on the ground fallen logs would be colonized by webs of fungal strands, and breakdown of the tree would proceed apace. Insects and other invertebrates contributed to the process, excavating tunnels to attack the wood itself or to eat the fungi and bacteria that were in it. Gradually the log would be weakened; it lost its shape and all that would be left was a line of nettles

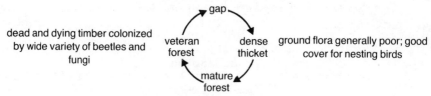

butterflies and other sun-loving
insects; plants of the wood edge

gap

dead and dying timber colonized
by wide variety of beetles and
fungi

veteran
forest

dense
thicket

ground flora generally poor; good
cover for nesting birds

mature
forest

ground flora and shrub layer re-
form; different bird species use
different layers (see below)

Changes in use by wildlife as the trees grow.

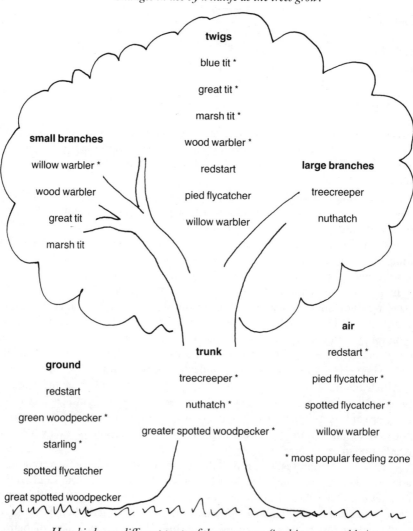

twigs

blue tit *

great tit *

marsh tit *

small branches

wood warbler *

willow warbler *

redstart

large branches

wood warbler

pied flycatcher

treecreeper

great tit

willow warbler

nuthatch

marsh tit

trunk

air

ground

treecreeper *

redstart *

redstart

nuthatch *

pied flycatcher *

green woodpecker *

greater spotted woodpecker *

spotted flycatcher *

starling *

willow warbler

spotted flycatcher

* most popular feeding zone

great spotted woodpecker

How birds use different parts of the same tree (in this case an alder).

showing where its nutrients had temporarily enriched the soil. However, while it remained above ground the log provided a safe site where tree seedlings could establish; a place where mosses and liverworts could grow without being shaded by the surrounding herbs and grasses; the log may have been used as a pathway for small mammals moving through the forest; and other animals burrowed underneath it for shelter and food.

All the indications are that the wildwood was particularly rich in dead wood – logs on the ground and rotting stumps, standing dead trees and dead branches high in the canopy of living ones. Now we might describe such a stand as moribund because we view it in terms of the trees and what we can get from them. Shift the emphasis a little: look at the whole range of species in the system (including the hidden army of fungi), the number of inter-relationships between species and the efficiency of re-cycling of nutrients. Each type of dead wood provides for a different range of species. Modern managed forests, which lack this dead wood delight, are the poorer.

Where has all the wildwood gone?

The wildwood is no more. The first peoples who lived in our forests had little more effect on it than other large mammals such as beaver, boar and wild ox. Their trackways may have been concentrated on ridges of hills where the ground was drier, the forest perhaps a little more open and there was more chance of being able to see where you were going. However, once forests started to be cleared on a large scale for settled agriculture, then the nature of the remaining wildwood also changed and some of the effects were irreversible. We are less than ten generations of an oak away from the wildwood, but if you stand in the middle of Salisbury Plain or on the Cheviots it is hard to believe it ever existed.

Most of Britain has not been forest for hundreds, in some areas thousands, of years. Large tracts had been cleared before the Romans came and the process continued as populations grew and axes and ploughs improved. By the time of the Norman conquest woodland in southern Britain was sufficiently scarce as to be measurable on a parish-by-parish basis. So woods in the Domesday Book are described in terms of their size or the number of pigs that they might support when there was a good crop of acorns. Counties such as Cornwall which have little ancient woodland were often already poorly wooded in the eleventh century. More extensive woodland may have survived relatively undisturbed in the uplands of northern England, Wales and Scotland into the late medieval period. However even remote and isolated valleys in these regions once held small but long-established communities, who would have used the woodland resource on their doorstep.

The medieval 'forests', home of the king's deer, at one time extended over vast areas of England and had laws that (in theory) were quite oppressive. Large dogs might have three claws on their forefeet removed, and prior to the 13th century, you might be killed for killing a deer. But what good was a dead deer or a dead peasant to a monarch hundreds of miles away? I suspect that often the

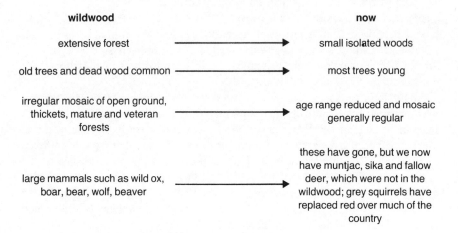

wildwood		now
extensive forest	⟶	small isolated woods
old trees and dead wood common	⟶	most trees young
irregular mosaic of open ground, thickets, mature and veteran forests	⟶	age range reduced and mosaic generally regular
large mammals such as wild ox, boar, bear, wolf, beaver	⟶	these have gone, but we now have muntjac, sika and fallow deer, which were not in the wildwood; grey squirrels have replaced red over much of the country

punishment for this and lesser offences became a fine. However, these 'Forests' were not all covered by trees, far from it, and the woods they did contain were likely to be managed. Almost every new study emphasizes the impact that our ancestors had on their surroundings and pushes back the time when woods were last truly 'wild'.

The forests that once grew in the fertile valley bottoms have been most completely destroyed. Almost nowhere in the lowlands do old forests of alder, black poplar and tall willows survive. Similarly only in a few places do woods stretch up towards what was once the natural tree-line. Perhaps the best example of the latter is at Creag Fhiaclach in the Cairngorms where stunted Scots pine grow at 610 m altitude. Other famous high altitude woods such as Wistman's Wood on Dartmoor or the Keskadale Oaks in the Lake District are much lower. Instead of forests forming the dominant feature in the landscape, isolated woods are surrounded by open farmland, towns and cities.

Of the inhabitants of the wildwood, some, such as blackbirds and foxes, have adapted very successfully to today's much changed countryside and now are found both in woods and out of them. Buzzards and golden eagles, which probably hunted in the more open parts of the wildwood, are now generally associated with the open moor. For other plants and animals conditions outside woods are very hostile indeed; they might almost be living on very small islands miles from anywhere in the middle of an ocean. They cannot spread easily from one wood to the next; if a large fire, major wind storm or forestry management wipes out their habitat on one site there is little chance that the wood will be recolonized from another in less than a century or two.

Some animals, such as the red squirrel, the capercaillie and a few butterflies, have indeed died out in places and have had to be re-introduced to particular woods or to Britain as a whole. Other large mammals have been eliminated completely. We cannot know the excitement that there is in seeing such beasts as wolves and bear (from a safe place) in the wild in Britain. There are no wild boar to disturb the soil, to break up dense mats of grass and bracken and help create seedbeds for regeneration. They have left a gap in the ecosystem such that it no longer works quite as it did previously.

Other species have been introduced to places where they did not occur before or have increased to the point where they are virtually out of control. Deer – both native roe and red and introduced fallow, muntjac and sika – are more common than at any time in recent history. They eat saplings and coppice regrowth in the woods and so prevent regeneration in many small gaps. Grey squirrels strip the bark from young trees which means the future of beechwoods is much more uncertain than in the past.

Woods are tidier and their growth more controlled. Trees are cut before they are really old and dead wood is removed. Gaps are mostly created where and when the forester wishes them to occur and are of the sizes he or she determines, although occasionally the wind plays havoc with their plans. The stark standing root plates left when the trees were uprooted by the 1987 storm were a shock to many in the south-east of England, so long is it since they were a common characteristic feature of our woods.

Even in the ancient woods that are descended from the wildwood, consciously or unconsciously, foresters and land owners have been altering the distribution of different species. Lime was one of the commonest trees in the wildwood of southern Britain, but now it is quite unusual. The oak and ash that took over from lime on many sites as the woods started to be managed have themselves often been replaced this century by Norway spruce or larch.

A modern wildwood

We cannot restore or recreate the wildwood, but we can leave areas and see what happens when they are left to develop with as little interference from people as possible. (Visitors may have to be discouraged since there is a risk that large branches could fall and injure them.) This approach is being followed on some nature reserves.

Undisturbed areas, whether a whole wood or just one corner left alone, help us to understand the many ways in which we have altered our environment and continue to do so. We can compare such areas with nearby commercial plantations to see what effects management has. To identify where to leave woods alone and when to interfere long-term studies are essential in both managed and unmanaged woods. However, anyone with access to a piece of wood can learn much from just mapping it in detail and following the changes from year to year.

One of the first differences we might expect between an unmanaged and a managed wood is that there will be a build-up of dead wood and old trees; also the soil will not be disturbed by tractors and other modern machinery. We should also expect some surprises: it is impossible to predict in detail what will happen in a wood that is left to itself.

At Lady Park Wood (Gwent) beech looked set to dominate the canopy and had been growing better than other trees since the 1940s. However after the

1976 drought many beech died and the tree that is now taking over is the lime (the tree once so widespread in the wildwood). In the Black Wood of Rannoch (Perthshire) concern was expressed about the number of dead or apparently moribund trees – the whole wood seemed about to collapse and there was little regeneration. Thirty years on, the wood is still there and, ready to last out a few more decades of researchers, most of the trees that seemed so fragile are still growing. A steady growth of seedlings and saplings means that lack of regeneration is not the problem that it appeared.

It would be nice to think that it might be possible to restore some of the large mammals that we have lost, although it is hard to imagine how. But if the sea-eagle is now back as a breeding bird through a re-introduction programme, perhaps we might manage to find space for beavers, wolves or boar?

3

Shadows of the Wildwood

Scattered through the country are woods which do not appear to have been cleared in the last 400 years – the ancient woods. Some are direct descendants of the wildwood. They are on land that has borne trees in an unbroken succession back to the times when a red squirrel might have travelled from one side of the country to another without touching the ground. Other ancient woods do not go back quite as far but grew up on fields and commons abandoned in Roman or medieval times. Although they lack a direct link to the wildwood there has been time for trees to grow up and die several times; for the woods to be exposed to the range of British weather including rare events such as the 1987 storm or the 1976 drought; even for those species that spread to and through woods very slowly to have crept in. These species have themselves often come to be used as 'indicators' of ancient woodland; where some of these plants (usually at least five species, but sometimes forty or fifty) occur in a wood, this is taken as an indication that it is probably ancient, even in the absence of other evidence. Since these species are much rarer in other woods, ancient woods are generally much richer than recent woodland upstarts in the British landscape. Ancient woods have been identified in a variety of way – not just by their plants. Most should be shown on the full range of maps produced from the seventeenth century on, although some do get omitted. Less often you can find them referred to in legal documents (wills and court cases), charters or descriptions of journeys. The woods themselves may provide a clue. They are often surrounded by old earth banks (replaced by walls in the north-west) and contain large old coppice stools.

In a country as thickly populated as ours, how does it happen that land stays in one use for so long? There are places like the Geary Ravine on Skye which are so steep and inaccessible that it is hard to imagine anyone ever wanting to clear them for agriculture and the effort involved in cutting the hazel or birch would hardly be worth the firewood. These are the exceptions. Most ancient woods survive because for most of their existence they have produced something that was needed, be it charcoal, boat timbers or acorns for pigs. How the woods were treated depended on what that something was.

For the most part the ancient woods that made it through to the twentieth century were treated as coppice or coppice with standards. Locally some, such as the native pinewoods of Scotland, grew and were managed as 'high forests' where trees were allowed to grow to their full heights. Particularly in the south, there were areas that were important for grazing as well as timber – wood pastures – where the trees might be pollarded. (These last are dealt with in chapter 8).

These different forms of management changed the appearance and composition of ancient woods compared to the natural forest, the wildwood, and had a profound influence on which plants and animals could continue to live in them. Coppicing led to more openings in the forest and so favoured the plants that grew in woodland gaps, glades and along woodland edges. The veteran pollards found in wood pastures allowed many lichens and dead wood beetles to thrive. Where such woods have escaped the replanting with conifers that has been common forestry practice in the last fifty years their composition often mirrors what would have been found in the forests of the past. They may not be wholly natural, only semi-natural, but they are shadows of the wildwood.

The ancient woodland pattern

Ancient semi-natural woodland varies in its abundance and composition from county to county, reflecting in part the natural influences of soil and climate that shaped the wildwood, but bearing also the imprint of our ancestors. In parts of the Weald of Kent, Sussex and Surrey, for instance, the cover of ancient woodland at about 20 per cent is almost as much as the average for central Europe; other concentrations occur in the Wye Valley, the southern Lake District and Deeside; but in many other areas ancient woodland is scarce or absent.

Some of the gaps in the current distribution are areas that may never have had woodland at all, such as the top of the Cairngorms and the boglands of Caithness and Sutherland. The great southern wetlands of the Fens, Somerset Levels and Pevensey Levels, are devoid of ancient woods as are the low-lying coastal plains of the Lancashire coast to the Solway Firth. Formerly these last were covered by extensive raised bogs.

Perhaps little ancient woodland survives on the chalk lands of southern England because the original forests were fairly open and relatively easy for Bronze and Iron Age peoples to clear. The same may also be true for forests on poor soils elsewhere, such as those of the Brecklands, south Dorset and parts of the uplands of west and north Britain, where there is evidence of early

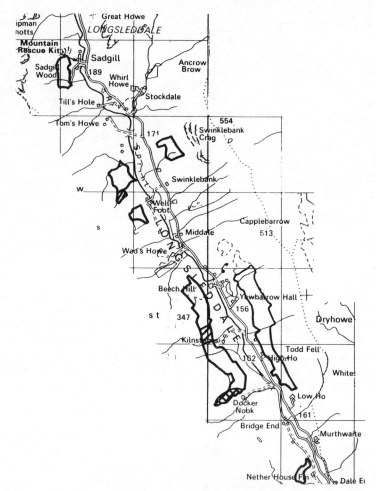

Ancient woods on the valleysides in Longsleddale (Cumbria) (Crown Copyright).

settlements. On poor, acid soils forest clearance could lead to a further loss of such nutrients as the soil did hold, so that heather and other heathy plants spread. Once formed, heath and moor could then be maintained fairly easily by grazing and periodic fires which would kill any tree seedlings.

Elsewhere most parishes had woods but they might be pushed back to the outskirts of the parish, as seems to have occurred in the area east of Oxford, to the poorest soils, or the steep mid slopes as at Long Sleddale (Cumbria), between the rich valley bottom fields and the upper pastures. Otherwise firewood and building timbers would have to be brought in which might be inconvenient as well as expensive.

The parish woods were owned (often by the Lord of the Manor) and highly valued especially where they were scarce. Local people might have the right to collect firewood 'by hook or by crook' – quite specific instructions in those days, not the free-for-all expression of current usage – and sometimes to take timber for repairing houses, waggons, etc. Unauthorized wood-cutting within the woods was treated seriously; for example, in 1256 Henry de Bethum accused Roger de Lancaster of taking 200 trees from his wood at Halecat (in the southern Lake District – the woods are still there, despite the loss) and this sort of court case is frequent in medieval records.

Ancient woodland has indeed often survived best where it was being cut regularly, where there were thriving industries that made use of the wood produced. Among such well wooded places are parts of North Wales and Argyll where oak was grown to produce charcoal for smelting iron while its bark was used in the tanning of leather. Further south, the characteristic landscape of the Chilterns derives in part from the use of the beechwoods to provide timber for furniture making.

Quirks of ownership have also influenced the likelihood of ancient woods surviving. Woods are often most at risk when they acquire a new owner or manager determined to leave his or her mark on the place. Woods that are on large estates or are part of crown land have generally remained for long periods in one ownership. They are more likely to have been kept under reasonably stable management. The owner of a small estate or farm often faced more pressure to clear the wood completely, because he or she had no other land available. On the other hand, large estates have also sometimes been guilty of neglect and clearance; they often had the resources other land owners did not for completely altering the character of ancient woods by replanting them (next chapter).

Owners, even if they are the crown, are not the only people with rights in a piece of woodland and this has both helped and hindered the survival of ancient woods. At the least it makes major changes in land use more complicated, because several parties need to agree the change. Such rights (apart from that of collecting firewood) might include the collection of bracken or leaf mould for bedding, the taking of peat, cutting hay from any glades or grassy places, the right to turn out pigs when there was an acorn crop or to graze livestock in the wood. These rights played an important part in the medieval agricultural system, although they were later abandoned or bought out over much of the country. The sharing of power between owners and the commoners with rights to graze cattle, ponies or sheep is a major reason why there are still woods in some former royal hunting forests such as Hatfield (Essex) and the New Forest (Hampshire). If the owner wanted to clear the wood, the commoners were likely to try to prevent it and vice versa.

Thus for a variety of reasons individual woods have individual histories: Hayley Wood in Cambridgeshire has remained remarkably stable in shape and size in the last 700 years apart from a small recent addition at its northern end; Strathfarrar Woods (Inverness) have shown a gradual decline in their total area since the middle of the eighteenth century and have become much fragmented; by contrast in Wytham Woods (Oxfordshire) what were separate blocks of ancient woodland have become linked through new planting and natural regeneration on old common land.

INDICATOR SPECIES

No plant is a perfect indicator of ancient woodland, but the following fifty species seem to have the strongest affinities for ancient woodland over the widest range. Locally other species have been suggested for particular regions – creeping soft grass (*Holcus mollis*), for example, in southern England – but these could not be used elsewhere. The number of indicator species found in a wood is affected by its size, soil type and management and by how much time you put into the survey as well as its history. Thus we can only say that the more of the species that are present the more likely the wood is to be ancient, but there are no upper or lower limits beyond which a wood either definitely is or is not ancient.

Small-leaved lime *Tilia cordata*
Wild service tree *Sorbus torminalis*
Birds-nest orchid *Neottia nidus-avis*
Early purple orchid *Orchis mascula*
Herb Paris *Paris quadrifolia*
Lily of the valley *Convallaria majalis*
Sweet woodruff *Galium odoratum*
Hairy woodrush *Luzula pilosa*
Pendulous sedge *Carex pendula*
Remote sedge *Carex remota*
Smooth stalked sedge *Carex laevigata*
Wood melick *Melica uniflora*
Wood millet *Milium effusum*
Butchers broom *Ruscus aculeatus*
Wood goldilocks *Ranunculus auricomus*
Midland hawthorn *Crataegus oxyacanthoides*
Hay-scented buckler fern *Dryopteris aemula*
Columbine *Aquilegia vulgaris*

Nettle leaved bell-flower *Campanula trachelium*
Crab apple *Malus sylvestris*
Cow wheat *Melampyrum pratense*
Early dog violet *Viola reichenbachiana*
Moschatel *Adoxa moschatellina*
Sanicle *Sanicula europaea*
Three veined sandwort *Moehringia trinervia*
Wood speedwell *Veronica montana*
Wood spurge *Euphorbia amygdaloides*
Bearded couch *Agropyron caninum*
Giant fescue *Festuca gigantea*
Hairy brome *Bromus ramosus*
Wood meadow grass *Poa nemoralis*
Wood sedge *Carex sylvatica*
Wood club rush *Scirpus sylvaticus*
Field maple *Acer campestre*
Southern wood-rush *Luzula forsteri*

Species which are useful indicators in the south and east but less good in the west:

Barren strawberry *Potentilla sterilis*
Greater butterfly orchid *Platanthera chloranthera*
Primrose *Primula vulgaris*
Wood anemone *Anemone nemorosa*
Wood sorrel *Oxalis acetosella*
Wood vetch *Vicia sylvatica*
Yellow archangel *Lamiastrum galeobdolon*
Yellow pimpernel *Lysimachia nemorum*

Greater wood-rush *Luzula sylvatica*
Pale sedge *Carex pallescens*
Hard fern *Blechnum spicant*
Golden scaled buckler fern *Dryopteris borreri*
Wood horsetail *Equisetum sylvaticum*
Pignut *Conopodium majus*
Wild daffodil *Narcissus pseudonarcissus*

Why is big beautiful?

The wildwood stretched for miles, but now few ancient woods measure more than one mile in any direction. Most cover less than ten hectares. This matters because large woods are particularly important for nature conservation. The

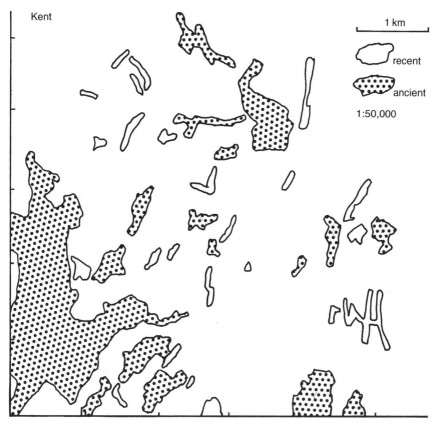

Kent

1 km

recent

ancient

1:50,000

The Weald of Kent: still an area with large ancient woods.

larger the wood the more species it contains and there can be more individuals of each of those species. For example, one oak tree can provide food for many winter moth caterpillars. However, the blue tits that feed on the caterpillars need several such trees in their territories to be assured of an adequate food supply for their young. In turn one pair of blue tits and young would not provide much of a meal for a sparrow-hawk, so these must have larger areas of woodland in which to hunt.

Even in a completely natural forest plants and animals would have died out at one place from time to time. For instance there might have been species that fed on oak, and the oaks then might have been shaded out by faster growing beech. Such local extinctions still occur in ancient woods, caused by exceptional events (drought, disease or storms) and through the changes that occur regularly as part of the management cycle. In a large wood, however, the species usually survives elsewhere and so can recolonize the patches from which it has been lost. Where the woodland has been split into many small fragments and a species has been lost from one of them there is the initial difficulty of getting the species back into the wood before it can spread through it.

Finally, we do not know enough about whether there is a loss of genetic

The Cotswold plateau (Gloucestershire).   Most of the surviving woods are small.

diversity through in-breeding in the isolated populations of plants and animals that exist in small woods. Maintaining genetic diversity and hence the potential to adapt to changing conditions could become much more important to the survival of our native wildlife, if, as seems likely, our climate is going to change in the next century.

Where only a few big ancient woods remain, these tend to be the focus of attention for nature conservation efforts, but we must not ignore small woods in the process. There are many places where it is the scatter of small woods that are the last refuges for our original woodland wildlife. Small woods also survive on soils and in situations where a large wood would have been cleared. They can contain features and species that are not found elsewhere. The balance between large and small woods helps to create the distinctive character of our landscapes and their wildlife, and so is worth retaining. The Weald of Kent and Speyside, for example, are districts where most of the ancient woods are large, whereas Powys and Northumberland and the rolling landscape of eastern Gloucestershire are characterized by a scatter of small woods.

Trees and shrubs

The distribution of species from north-west Scotland to Kent is comparable to the spread of species after the last ice age – with the most inhospitable areas being equated with the earliest periods after the ice. So in parts of north-west Scotland, especially on the Hebridean islands, the only native woodland consists of open willow and sometimes birch-hazel scrub. Wind and salt spray prune back new shoots that stick above the shelter of their neighbours.

On the mainland, where conditions are more sheltered, proper woods exist, of birch, aspen and rowan with scattered alder on wet ground and hazel where the soils are richer. In the central Highlands, where our coldest winters occur, pine and juniper are common and the woods have an affinity with those of Scandinavia.

Further south, oaks, ash and once elm form the main canopy with an increasing number of other shrubs and tree species below them. The sessile oak is usually associated with woods of western Britain and with sandy soils, while the pedunculate oak occurs more in the south-east and on clay soil. However there is much overlap in their ranges and they may hybridize so a clear distinction in their distribution cannot be made.

Beech and hornbeam appear only in the semi-natural stands of southern England and Wales, which are related to those of northern France and Belgium. Our woods are thus the western ends of two chains of variation – that coming through central and southern Europe, which is mainly broadleaved, and that through northern Europe, which is mainly coniferous – but they also have distinctive elements of their own, because they are at the end of their respective chains. The abundance of ash-dominated woods on limestone, the dense understorey of holly found in western woods and abundant yew are some of the features that mark out our woods from those of continental Europe.

Within any one area the natural composition of the ancient woods reflects local differences in the soil. Wet ground is distinguished by the abundance of alder, willow and, if it is peaty, downy birch. Dry acid soils tend to be poor in trees and shrubs, but through most of the country oaks and birches are common. In the south they are joined by beech as in the New Forest, while Scots pine is important in the central Highlands.

As the soils get richer the change is usually reflected first in the ground flora: bramble, honeysuckle and creeping soft-grass are added to or replace the bilberry, bracken and wavy hair-grass of the most acid woods. Apart from an increase in the amount of hazel present there may not be much change in the tree and shrub mixture. However in woods on the richest soils, ash and elm and in the south shrubs such as dogwood, privet and spindle occur with the more widespread hazel and hawthorn. Dog's mercury often forms a green carpet and is particularly noticeable in the spring because it is one of the first plants to emerge as winter loses its grip.

Large variations in soil and climate within our relatively small country produce considerable differences between our ancient woods, but historical factors also have an important influence.

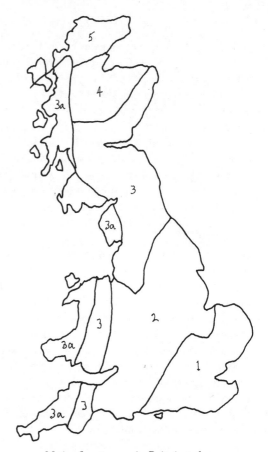

1. **South-eastern mixed woods.**
Oak, ash and field maple
generally common, joined by
beech and hornbeam and
introduced sweet chestnut.
2. **Midland mixed woods.** Oak,
ash and field maple common;
hornbeam, sweet chestnut
scarce.
3. **Upland woods.** Sessile oak
generally commonest, alder
abundant on richer or wetter soil.
3a. **Atlantic zone.** Similar to 3,
but woods generally richer in
mosses and liverworts.
4. **Highland.** Pine and birch
predominate.
5. **North-west.** Most woods birch
and birch/hazel stands.

Major forest zones in Britain today.

Why is small-leaved lime so scarce when it was a dominant tree in the
wildwood over much of southern Britain? It is very long-lived and can be
maintained almost indefinitely by coppicing, but its leaves and bark are quite
palatable which makes it susceptible to grazing. One difference between groups
of woods, such as those in Lincolnshire or Suffolk, where lime remains
abundant, and other ancient woods nearby on similar soils where it is absent
may be that the latter were at some time grazed. But why has it not come back
into those woods where it appears conditions are still right for its growth?
Climate change plays a part – our summers are not as warm as they were some
5,000 years ago when lime spread to its current limits. Now it seldom sets viable
seed in the north of its range. Lime might even benefit from global warming if
this led to warmer summers in Britain. In the south seeds and seedlings are
produced but the seedlings are, like the mature tree, very palatable and are
quickly eaten by voles and mice. Presumably voles ate lime seedlings in the
wildwood also, but perhaps then limes fruited much more freely so that at least
one or two of the seedlings in any gap would get away; perhaps they relied less
on seedlings to produce new trees than on slow spread outwards as branches

that were in contact with the soil formed roots and so eventually a new tree. Either way once lime was lost from a wood it rarely came back because successful regeneration and spread by seed were so rare.

The dominance of sessile oak in woods in the west poses another question. Studies of pollen deposits and historical accounts suggest that the wildwood of these areas used to be more mixed, but if so, where have the other trees and shrubs gone? Sessile oak was probably always one of the commonest trees in these woods, but because it was so valuable for charcoal and tanbark it was encouraged and other species – birch, rowan and holly – eliminated when the woods were cut. Beech has similarly been favoured in the Chilterns during the last 150 years for the furniture trade; and it is no coincidence that hornbeam, which provides good fuel, forms such a major part of the woods around London.

Recently the composition of our ancient woods has been changing again as large elms have died from Dutch elm disease. Their gaunt ivy shrouded skeletons stand as silent memorials. Some woods in eastern England lost most of their tree cover as a result. The consequences were less drastic where elm was mixed with ash and other trees, but even so large glades, often taken over by nettles and elder, have been created. A hopeful sign is the amount of young elm regrowth from suckers or old stumps. Some of this will die in its turn when the poles are large enough to attract the bark beetle that spreads the fungus that causes the disease, but perhaps some will survive to form a new generation of stately elms.

Ancient woods are also changing through the spread of sycamore and rhododendron which were introduced by our immediate ancestors. Moist soils rich enough for ash or elm are favoured by sycamore, while rhododendron is most aggressive in the wet acid woods of the west.

Centuries of intervention have thus left their marks on the tree and shrub layer of ancient semi-natural woods, but environmental factors have played an even greater part in shaping the distribution of the other plants and animals in a wood because usually these have been left to fend for themselves.

Plants that live in our semi-natural woods

There is a broad north-west/south-east division in the distribution of many plants of the woodland floor, connected with the same climatic differences that influenced the trees and shrubs. Flowers restricted to or more common in the north and west include chickweed wintergreen, globeflower, Welsh poppy and melancholy thistle. Others such as herb Paris, nettle-leaved bellflower and oxlip have their stronghold in the south-east.

Brambles can grow on a wide range of soils and so do some of our commonest woodland plants, but most species are more restricted. Those occurring may suggest the soil conditions present. In many Welsh oakwoods a regular pattern can often be seen. Bilberry and wavy hair-grass on the steep rocky slopes indicate that the soil is probably shallow and acid; towards the bottom there is more sweet vernal-grass, creeping soft-grass and bent-grasses with herbs such as tormentil which suggest that the soils are deeper here and a little richer; while further down dog's mercury and enchanter's nightshade are signs of quite fertile conditions formed by the washing of soil nutrients to the bottom of the slope.

In dry ash and beechwoods patches of moist rich soil may be picked out in spring by an overwhelming stench of wild garlic. Stands of meadowsweet, opposite-leaved golden saxifrage and creeping buttercup are better avoided unless you are wearing Wellington boots, because often they occur on very wet ground in woods.

Mosses, liverworts and some ferns are particularly sensitive to drying out. Britain has some of the best woods for these plants in Europe with many rare species, because our rainfall is heavier and more evenly spread through the year than most of continental Europe. The best woods for these are in the wet west, although outliers occur in the shaded gills (narrow valleys) of south-east England. Within woods the richest areas are usually those that have been least disturbed; a continuous canopy of trees helps to keep up the humidity levels. Perhaps these moisture-loving species were once more widespread before woods were felled or coppiced at frequent intervals. Now it is only in the wettest places that the most sensitive species remain common.

More widespread are deep carpets of the robust species of moss such as *Leucobryum glaucum*, which forms hemispherical cushions, which may reach more than thirty centimetres across. So abundant may some of these mosses be at the best sites that they have been collected and sold for packing and for flower arrangements. This can cause much damage to the wood since the rates at which the mosses regrow are very slow. Mosses can grow even in deep shade and around the base of beech trees there is often a distinctive moss zone where the poor light and competition for water from the beech roots prevent flowering plants establishing. Water running off the beech trunk provides enough moisture for the mosses to grow. The species found in this zone are frequently those of acid soils, regardless of the surroundings, because the water becomes more acid as it runs down the beech trunks. The direction in which the water runs off most frequently influences the degree of moss cover. Thus mosses are not found only on the north side of trees, contrary to popular belief, although there is an element of sense behind this. The north side is shaded from the sun and so moister and better for moss growth.

Moss and liverworts may share the tree trunks and rocks with lichens. Some of these also require the moist conditions of the west, but many can tolerate, indeed need, fairly light and dry conditions. During the last hundred years all but a few hardy species disappeared from most woods in eastern Britain as a result of air pollution carried by the prevailing south-westerly winds from major towns and factories. Species that used to be common in Epping Forest have declined or disappeared since the mid-nineteenth century. Some species seem to need large old trees, probably because the nature of the bark is different from that in young trees. Such old trees are scarce in managed woods. So many of the best sites for lichens, some of the best in Europe, are old parks rather than closed canopy woods.

. . . and animals

Because plants are affected by regional variations, so in turn are the animals that live on them. Several of the fritillary butterflies and the hairstreaks are largely restricted to the south because they need particularly warm sites for their caterpillars to develop. The black hairstreak is even more closely confined to part of the Midland clay belt, although this is also related to past management that allowed the growth of tall blackthorn, the butterfly's host plant. By contrast, the chequered skipper, having died out in England, was rediscovered living in open woods on the west coast of Scotland. There are other northern specialists such as the Cousin German moth that feeds on heather, bilberry and low saplings of birch in Scotland. The ranges of northern and southern species of wood ant overlap in the valleys of the Lake District, just as does the distribution of many plants. It is probably significant that the southern species is found on the limestone outcrops around Morecambe Bay since such woods, being very free-draining, are often relatively warm. In the Duddon Valley on more acid, moist soils, the northern species was reported.

Warm-blooded animals can usually tolerate a wider range of climatic conditions and are more likely to travel over wide distances, but they may still be restricted by regional patterns in the structure and composition of the woods. The nightingale, which feeds and nests in fairly dense scrubby conditions, is largely a bird of south-east England and often associated with worked coppice. Wood-warbler, redstart and pied flycatcher are more characteristic of grazed western oakwoods which provide the open space below the canopy where the flycatcher feeds and the relatively bare woodland floor for the wood-warbler to nest on. In fact the pied flycatcher can live where there is a dense shrub layer, but in such woods blue tits are usually common and are likely to occupy possible nest sites first. Northern pinewoods are home to capercaillie, crested tit and Scottish crossbill.

There are more species of bat in the south because the flying insects on which they feed are more abundant. On the other hand many of the large carnivores (wildcat, polecat and pine marten) were driven out of southern and eastern woods by persecution and are only slowly spreading back. These animals are not linked directly to a particular type of woodland but need cover to hide in and a good supply of food (mainly small mammals and birds). Thus they are most likely to occur in broadleaved or mixed woods or old conifer areas where there is enough light for ground and shrub layers to flourish.

Red squirrels survive in only a few places in the south such as the Isle of Wight. Their range contracted sharply this century and in much of the country their place has been taken by greys. The grey squirrel, first released in England about a century ago, seems to be much more effective than the red at exploiting broadleaved woodland. Greys take unripe hazel nuts and can also thrive on acorns whereas the red squirrel uses ripe hazels that have fallen to the ground and cannot digest acorns as well. If the two occur together in a broadleaved wood the red is gradually displaced.

What you find in an ancient wood thus depends on where you are, which is

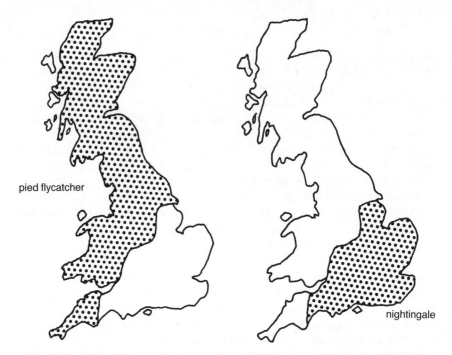

Contrasting distributions of pied flycatcher and nightingale: the pied flycatcher needs fairly open woods for its feeding flights below the canopy. Hence it is abundant in grazed western oak woods. The nightingale on the other hand nests in fairly dense scrubby areas and was particularly common in worked coppice.

an important point if we are to conserve the full range of our woodland wildlife. We must look after woods across the whole country, not just in one or two regions. This happily coincides with the desirability of making wildlife accessible to people rather than something they must drive miles to see.

Climate and soil help to explain much of the variation in the composition of ancient woods, but when their structure is examined the effects of differences in past and present management are more important.

Coppice systems

Many ancient woods were managed by coppicing. In Scotland the evidence of a coppice tradition prior to the seventeenth century is patchy compared with that for England and Wales, but even here there are records for particular woods showing that coppicing was a regular practice in medieval times. Our understanding of how the woods were worked comes from their structure, the remains of the industries that used the woodland produce, from old descriptions and particularly from complaints when things went awry. Trade directories and newspapers from the nineteenth century testify to the number of people in rural parishes who worked in or depended on their local woods.

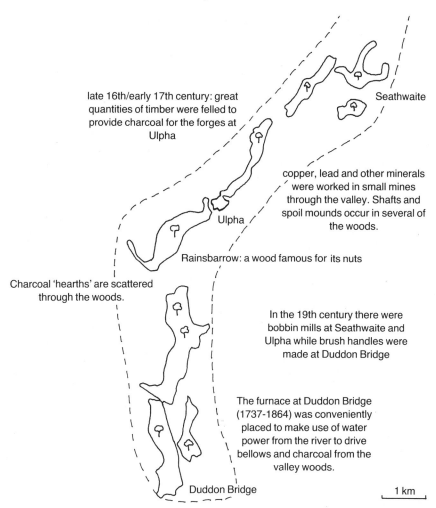

late 16th/early 17th century: great
quantities of timber were felled to
provide charcoal for the forges at
Ulpha

Seathwaite

copper, lead and other minerals
were worked in small mines
through the valley. Shafts and
spoil mounds occur in several of
the woods.

Ulpha

Rainsbarrow: a wood famous for its nuts

Charcoal 'hearths' are scattered
through the woods.

In the 19th century there were
bobbin mills at Seathwaite and
Ulpha while brush handles were
made at Duddon Bridge

The furnace at Duddon Bridge
(1737-1864) was conveniently
placed to make use of water
power from the river to drive
bellows and charcoal from the
valley woods.

Duddon Bridge

1 km

Woods and industry in the Duddon Valley, Cumbria.

Usually the cutting was carefully controlled. For example in 1799 the Duke
of Argyll offered for sale eleven hags (patches of woodland for cutting) and it
was a condition of sale that the purchaser sold the timber to the Argyll Furnace
Company to be cut and made into charcoal, or the purchaser might make it into
charcoal himself and deliver the same to the company by whom he should be
paid at prices specified in the contract with the Duke.

A regular yield of poles, firewood, bark and other products might be
maintained from coppicing for centuries. The Duddon Valley, Cumbria, seems
to have produced iron using charcoal from the local woods from at least
medieval times until the late nineteenth century. It could be very profitable. In
1803 a visitor noted that the proprietors of Colton in south Cumbria 'had
ceased to breed sheep, so far were they involved in the cultivation of coppices'.
Early records suggest that there were also times when there was an export trade.

In the reign of Edward III merchants from France and Flanders were entering the port of Winchelsea (Kent) and plying up the river Rother in search of firewood. Larger trees, standards or perhaps parkland trees, were also sent abroad. By the king's orders 700 planks were sent in 1172 to Ireland from the forest of Inglewood (between Carlisle and Penrith).

There might be periods of neglect when the trees were left long beyond the normal cutting age: orderly cutting of the woods and protection of the regrowth were not always the case. If fences were not properly maintained (perhaps because of some dispute about grazing rights) the regrowth would be slow or patchy. A writer on the management of oak coppice in Scotland in 1874 notes an occasion when 'a flock of sheep had been allowed to stray for a few hours into a part of a two year old oak coppice, and this portion, though growing on the best soil . . . had a most cankered appearance and did not thrive nearly so well for three years as the uninjured part did.'

In the uplands, where much of the cutting was for charcoal or tanbark rather than local firewood or fencing, whole woods may have been felled at a time, with less concern given to maintaining the productivity of the site.

Nevertheless, almost all kinds of our native broadleaves as well as some introduced trees such as sweet chestnut and sycamore have been coppiced somewhere and the system seems to have proved suitable for managing woods across a wide range of conditions to meet the needs of local and national markets. What effect did it have on the wildlife?

Worked coppice is very different from the wildwood, but many plants and animals were able to flourish in these conditions. In particular, species that like open glade conditions such as butterflies could always find a newly cut patch nearby, as shade from the 'stool' (stump that has been coppiced) regrowth led to a previously cut area becoming unsuitable for them. Flowers bloomed in profusion in the years immediately following a cut; their seeds would become buried in the soil waiting the opportunity to grow when the coppice was next felled. The coppice stools themselves may have had their lives prolonged by this process; it is believed that some of the oldest such individuals may be over a thousand years old.

There is more open space per unit area in a coppice than probably occurred in the wildwood, so for some plants and animals coppice provided even better conditions than an equal area of wildwood. Wild daffodils, for example, thrive best where there are periods of alternating light and shade. This variation did occur in the natural forests but in an irregular fashion. In worked coppice the opening up of the wood (providing the light conditions) happened every 5 to 20 years. In Brigsteer Woods (Cumbria) a long history of coppicing has thus produced dramatic daffodil displays. Coppicing also produced a dense hazel shrub layer in many woods – probably denser than that found through much of the wildwood. For dormice this was a double blessing – the hazel nuts provided it with more food while the intertwining branches gave it the aerial pathways through the wood that it prefers.

It was just as well that many species were favoured by worked coppice given that the area of ancient semi-natural woodland now is only 1-2 per cent of the country compared to what had been 80 per cent cover for the wildwood. Quarts of some wildwood species could be squeezed into pint-pot sized woods only because of the variety produced by the coppice system. Even in small woods there was generally open space from the most recent cuttings; dense thicket stands waiting to be cut; old coppice stools and perhaps veteran pollard trees on the wood boundaries that might be suitable for some deadwood insects.

Maintaining a diversity of woodland habitats is important, so a common nature conservation aim nowadays is to keep the coppice system going where it is still worked and restart the cycle where it has been abandoned for only a short time. Realization of the importance of maintaining the coppice cycle came just in time to save the heath fritillary, one of Britain's rarest butterflies, from becoming extinct in its former Kentish stronghold. This butterfly is reluctant to fly very far and had been reduced to just a few scattered colonies in the Blean Woods north of Canterbury. Careful study of its requirements and a programme of regular coppice cuts has enabled the numbers to be built up to a healthy level again.

Most of the old markets for the produce of a coppice wood, particularly the larger ones, have disappeared. In the parish of Witherslack, for example, in 1786, 24 out of 52 tradesmen had a direct connection with the woods. By 1850 the number had halved, with the number of specialist workers (colliers, chair-makers and basket-makers) being particularly badly hit. In the old county of Cumberland between 1850 and 1911 the numbers employed in the wood and timber trades dropped from 1,265 to 650. Many of the necessary skills and traditions were lost in the carnage of two world wars.

There is now little demand for oak bark for tanning leather, although a firm in Cornwall does still use it to make high quality gloves. Charcoal is still made on a small scale in south Cumbria, largely for barbecues, but this is as nothing to the 1,000 tons needed annually in the eighteenth and nineteenth centuries, just for the Bonawe Iron Furnace near Oban.

Worked coppice is still relatively common in the south-east, much of it sweet chestnut which finds a fairly ready sale for hop poles and fencing. Ironically this is generally the least interesting type of coppice for nature conservation, because the soils and ground flora are generally poor and the sweet chestnut (an introduced species) has replaced the native woods of oak, beech and hornbeam.

Other coppices are cut and sold for pulp. The paper mill at Sudbrook, in Gloucestershire, is currently increasing its intake of coppice poles, which may encourage woodland owners to start cutting their woods again. On the other hand the paper mill at Sittingbourne in Kent is reducing the amount it buys because a much higher proportion of recycled paper is being used instead. Campaigns to re-use paper which are desirable in the long term have had this unfortunate local conservation side effect. New markets must be found to take the place of pulpwood. Perhaps it will be a Kentish charcoal campaign.

While there may not be a big demand for coppice, there are many woods scattered throughout the country that are still cut on a small scale often by volunteers. Keeping up the coppice tradition sounds romantic. The British Trust for Conservation Volunteers and the County Wildlife or Naturalists'

Trusts often organize work parties that you may join to cut coppice on woodland reserves. Demonstrations of charcoal burning or wattle fence making are sometimes arranged at local agricultural shows and country fairs. Courses have been run where you can learn to make chair legs from green wood using a pole-lathe as did the bodgers and on some courses you may even stay in the wood while you do it. All good fun and fine for a few hours on a sunny afternoon, but coppicing is hard work and, for the woodmen out in the wet and cold (usually this was winter work), the romance would have worn thin.

Expanding the area of worked coppice would benefit nature conservation especially in the south of Britain; however, we need to find modern markets for the produce, adapt machinery and skills to make the process cheaper and more comfortable for the workers, and find the extra cash needed to pay for the environmental benefits that will come from a revival of coppice compared with other management.

The woods where reinstating coppice will be of most value are those that were worked as coppice previously and have been cut at least once in the last 50 years (often during the Second World War). These are most likely still to contain at least some of the plants and animals that thrive under coppice systems, particularly if the soils are quite rich. Old coppice woods can be recognized by the large stumps. If most of these stems are less than about 15-20 cm diameter, the coppice has probably been cut recently. Sometimes you can find what appear to be old stools, but each now has only one stem growing on it. As coppice became less profitable in the nineteenth and twentieth centuries, so some foresters cut all but one stem from the stool to allow the stem to grow up and form a large tree similar to those found in natural woods and managed 'high forests'.

High-forest systems

Coppice provides mainly small material and for the most part this was what the local communities and industries who used the wood wanted. However there has always been demand for larger trees, whether for ships, for the centre post of a windmill, the major roof timbers of a great barn or the massive supports of something like the octagon in Ely cathedral. Frequently the whole tree was used in the construction, roughly squared, rather than being sawn into planks. If you look at the beams in old barns or houses you can often see where the softer sapwood, even sometimes the bark, was left on.

In part needs for such timber were met by standard trees grown with the coppice, or from hedgerow and parkland trees. Even now much of the home-grown broadleaved timber, particularly large-diameter timber, that arrives in sawmills in Britain comes from hedges.

The ease with which large trees could be sawn up into planks improved with the spread of power-driven mills in the nineteenth and twentieth centuries. At the same time the demand for small wood (particularly for fuel) shrank. High-forest systems, where the trees were grown for longer, hence were bigger and more attractive to foresters, developed. In France conversion of coppice woods to high forest has been part of a deliberate national forest policy over a hundred years, but we have had no such grand design, not least because we have only had a national forest authority since 1919. So the process here has been more haphazard.

Ancient woods were neglected or deliberately encouraged to grow up as high forest, sometimes by thinning the coppice, sometimes by favouring new young trees. This altered the balance of species in woods because smaller trees and shrubs such as hazel might be shaded out, for example. Oak was favoured in many places, such as the Forest of Dean, while beech was promoted in the Chilterns. Elsewhere natural regeneration of whatever species were available filled the gaps created when the trees were felled. There were cases of planting of seed or saplings, but these would often (as now if plantations are not weeded) have been overtaken by the natural regrowth on the site.

In parts of the uplands such as North Wales most of the oakwoods are now high forest and there are few signs of a former coppice working, even where it is known to have existed. In the native pinewoods in Scotland a coppice regime would not have been feasible since these trees do not regrow from cut stumps. The other main tree of the central and northern Highlands, the birch, does coppice but its stump rots quickly and as it commonly regenerates from seed in cut areas there is less advantage in coppice. These woods again have probably often been treated as high forest. There have been fewer descriptions of precisely how they were managed. There must have been control of grazing animals, but what were the limitations on what could be cut and when?

What difference did it make whether woods were treated as coppice or high forest for the wildlife? Many of the species in ancient woods can survive under either coppice or high forest stands, although some of the spring flowers may not bloom so profusely in high forest. Species groups that live on old trees and dead wood, particularly fungi, beetles and flies, may be more abundant in high forest, but those that use the early open stages of coppice will find it more difficult to thrive since there is less open ground in most managed high forests. Thus the butterflies of open glades, particularly the fritillaries, have disappeared from many neglected woods this century. The speckled wood and white admiral which can tolerate more shaded conditions have remained more widespread and even increased in places. Warblers may decline in some woods because there is less of the dense understorey in which they prefer to nest, whereas robin, blackbird, great tit and blue tit tend to proliferate. If the trees are allowed to grow old enough they might start to develop the holes and rotten branches that provide food and shelter for nuthatches and woodpeckers.

Ancient woods could be abandoned as relics from a former time that have no productive use in modern society. Their value, however, is very high as habitats for wildlife and they are storehouses of information about how our forebears worked in the many sawpits, charcoal hearths, kilns, trackways and log chutes that they contain. Because the soils have usually never been ploughed they may preserve undisturbed even older traces, both human – such as Iron Age earthworks – and of natural origin – such as the thin surface deposits of fine earth that are found in some soils believed to date from immediate post-glacial times. There are ancient woods within easy reach of most people, each with a different history and composition that can be investigated quite simply.

The survival of ancient woods into the twentieth century is part accident, part conscious recognition of the value they held in former societies, even a kind of reverence for their dark mystery and splendour. Unfortunately the special character of these woods was not widely recognized in the three decades after the last world war, when the forest industry was expanding rapidly. Consequently the treatment that was recommended for ancient woods differed little from that for a ploughed field. Woods that had borne native broadleaves or Scots pine for centuries were cleared and converted to often dull plantations mainly of introduced conifers: more timber was produced, but at a high conservation cost.

4

Two Spruce in Place of One Oak

Coppicing of ancient woods continued as long as it met the needs of the land owners and those with rights to cut wood. But other ways of managing woods, for example as plantations, were known and from the seventeenth century onwards books were produced that dealt with how land owners might grow more timber. There was no national training school for foresters however until the end of the last century, nor was there much interest or encouragement from the government for forestry development.

This changed, largely as a consequence of the First World War and the effects of the submarine blockade which disrupted imports. Britain imported over 90 per cent of its timber at this time so that massive fellings were needed in such woods to compensate for lost imports. The Forestry Commission, formed in 1919, initiated major planting programmes to avoid a repeat of this situation, but the new forests planted on open ground, for example around Thetford in Norfolk, were still too young to provide much timber during the Second World War. The trees growing in ancient woods were again felled on a large scale for the war effort. Afterwards many woods looked to be in a poor state. The 1947 Census of Woodland had a special category – 'devastated' – to describe those woods whose usable timber had been removed, and which had then been largely left.

As part of the process of rebuilding the country after the war owners were encouraged to improve the production of timber from both these and from other broadleaved woods. The replacement of generally slow growing, poor quality broadleaves with spruce and pine or conifer-broadleaved plantations was a logical move. Large areas of our native pinewoods were also replanted with faster growing species such as spruce. All this was supported by government policies and grants. There were sometimes complaints, but any opposition tended to be weak and ill-organized. In 1949 wildlife conservation was not a high priority for most people, and anyway the main threats to wildlife were expected to come from urban developments, not from agriculture and forestry. The extent to which these industries would develop and so alter the landscape was not anticipated.

The success (in timber productions terms) of the post-war forestry policies is reflected in the 40 per cent or so of ancient woods that are now covered by plantations, most of which have been established in the last 50 years. This is particularly noticeable in large woods. The process can be followed in the stock map for Salcey Forest in Northamptonshire, which records what trees were planted and when in each part of the wood. The forest, formerly worked as coppice, had been converted to a high forest in the middle of the nineteenth century. It was dominated by oak, with a mixture of ash and hazel, when it was transferred early this century to the Forestry Commission, who have been responsible for its subsequent felling and replanting. The way that the pattern of this replanting has varied, almost decade by decade, shows the shifts in the foresters' approach to woodland management.

Mixtures of broadleaved trees, including some such as beech which had not been grown in the forest previously, were tried in the 1930s, but there was a shift to oak-spruce mixes in the 1940s. A narrow broadleaved fringe around the edge of the new plantation area was often left to mask the scale of the felling. Later increasing amounts of spruce and less oak were used and the idea of leaving fringes was abandoned. Pure conifers were the fashion in the '60s as the pressures to make forestry more profitable increased. Then a swing back to mixtures and even pure broadleaves took place in the '80s in response to an increased concern for the landscape and wildlife value of broadleaved woodland. This is likely to be emphasized even more in the '90s. Foresters, like everyone else, are subject to fashions and changes of policy, but the effects of their actions are more long-lasting.

Oaks were planted in Salcey Forest in the early nineteenth century, but in many ancient woods regeneration had previously been largely from natural seedlings or coppice regrowth. So when modern forestry methods were brought into these woods, not only the species changed: there was a complete change of approach. Larger areas were cut at one time; centuries-old stumps were grubbed out or killed by herbicides; in many woods the ground was ploughed for the first time in its history. As the planted trees grew there was concern about the dark forbidding appearance of spruce and pine stands where there had previously been sheets of bluebells under oak, ash and hazel.

Some of the complaints were overstated; the ancient woodland flora and fauna has proved more resilient than either conservationists or foresters expected. Many plants and animals, while reduced in abundance, have hung on in replanted woods, ready to come back in force if conditions improve.

Whether a wood is coppiced or clear felled it looks much the same immediately afterwards. However in a coppice, or a wood managed by natural regeneration, the new crop that subsequently develops is directly descended from the old one.

It grows up from the old stumps or from seed shed by the trees that were there before. In some woods such links between generations may stretch back to the wildwood as we have seen in the previous chapter. In a plantation no such relationship need exist – the new crop can be and frequently is a totally different species of tree. That is seen as an advantage by many foresters since it gives them the chance to bring in faster-growing trees. But the local genetic strain of trees is lost and animals living on the former plants suddenly find themselves with no host.

In a plantation the distribution of young trees is not left to natural forces. Instead the forester places them exactly where he or she wishes them to go. Practical considerations usually mean that the trees are in lines or well defined groups so that they are easy to find and weed. Even where an effort at irregular spacing is made (and this rarely occurs in commercial woods) it is difficult to disguise the artificiality of the arrangement of trees in a young plantation.

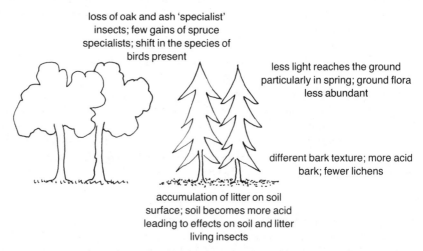

loss of oak and ash 'specialist' insects; few gains of spruce specialists; shift in the species of birds present

less light reaches the ground particularly in spring; ground flora less abundant

different bark texture; more acid bark; fewer lichens

accumulation of litter on soil surface; soil becomes more acid leading to effects on soil and litter living insects

Ways in which changing from oak and ash to a spruce crop affect the wildlife of a wood.

Occasionally the original trees are not completely eliminated, but survive on the edges of compartments. They may even threaten to outgrow the planted trees although in that case the forester is likely to clean them out at the first opportunity. Overall the individual relationship between the pattern of the trees and shrubs and a particular site is lost. In the past we could find oak-ashwoods in Cambridgeshire, hornbeams in Hertfordshire and sessile oaks in Clwyd and see a pattern in these distributions in terms of soil, climate or some past event, such as a severe drought or windblow. The occurrence of ash in some parts of a wood and beech in others, or of birch in some woods and pine in others in the Highlands could be explored with a view to finding a meaning in these differences. The plantations that have replaced such semi-natural woods tell us nothing about what may have been there in the past, or what may follow. They are like the numerous more-or-less identical housing estates that have been developed around old villages.

All change

Our native trees differ in the shade they cast, in the amount of leaf litter that they drop and whether it rots down quickly or not. The new crop in a plantation is unlikely to have the same characteristics as the species it replaces. As the new trees grow, they affect the distribution and abundance of the rest of the plants and animals in the wood. The greatest changes are likely when native broadleaved trees are replaced with introductions such as spruce.

The first obvious difference between deciduous broadleaves and evergreen conifers is the increased shade, a difference that is particularly noticeable in early spring. Many well loved wild flowers (bluebells, primroses and anemones) are growing rapidly at this season, because they can make use of the light reaching the forest floor before deciduous trees such as ash and oak come into leaf. Under evergreens there is no such boost of spring light and these flowers become less abundant.

Deciduous conifers, such as the larches, provide more opportunities for spring-flowering plants, but the thick litter layer that builds up under them, as under most of the evergreen conifers, smothers mosses and low-growing herbs. Where the litter is loose packed the roots of flowers such as wood sorrel and anemone dry out and they die.

Differences in the amount of leaf litter dropped and whether it is incorporated into the mineral soil or remains mainly on the surface alter the nature of the soil and the animals that live in it. The surface layers are generally more acid under conifers than under broadleaves, and particularly under young conifers. Springtails are more common among the surface litter layer produced under most conifers whereas earthworms, which are sensitive to soil acidity, are generally more common under broadleaves.

The differences between tree species are often very apparent when the planted trees are about 15-30 years old, when they form a dense thicket. By this time most of the shrubs, and the flowers and grasses of the woodland floor, have disappeared under conifers such as spruce, and only a few mosses may survive. The effects can be dramatic in mixtures where the trees have been planted as alternating bands of spruce and oak. Strips of green under the oak pick out where the plants hang on. Other refuges for the woodland flora may be patches where the planted trees have failed to grow or been blown over. Overall however less than 10 per cent of the ground is likely to be covered by vegetation under dense conifers compared to about 30 per cent or more under most of our native trees at this stage on the same site.

Fewer plants in and under the plantation means less cover and food for animals. The many insects that feed on our native trees and shrubs, particularly oak and willows, become less common. Only relatively few species, for example the moths, the mottled and winter beauties, have been able to transfer to the main trees planted in commercial plantations. The plant-feeding insects are particularly hard hit. At Bernwood Forest, Oxfordshire, overgrown coppice was much richer in moths than the adjacent conifer plantations. Some conifer specialists do come in including in this study the grey pine carpet and tawny barred angle, but only 3 per cent of the moths that were recorded fed on the conifers which make up the bulk of the forest. The shading out of the ground flora which had provided the food plants for most of the caterpillars was a major reason for the decline in both moth species and the number of individuals found.

New species have been attracted to the plantations, often insects that feed on the crop trees and which have been brought into Britain accidentally. Not all are welcome: some, such as the spruce bark beetle, have become pests. Some birds that favour coniferous trees, such as the goldcrest, have also increased. Other birds survive in plantations but have to alter the size and arrangement of their territories to take account of the changed food and cover provided by the new crop.

More light and more life

In a plantation 1,000–2,500 trees are usually planted on every hectare, whereas there is space enough for only 100–200 when the trees are 50–100 years old if they are to grow well. As the plantation ages, therefore, the trees are thinned, that is, some trees are cut out to provide more growing space for those remaining. The trees that are removed, the thinnings, are sold, where possible, to provide the first financial returns from the investment made when the trees were first planted.

A similar thinning out of young trees happens in natural woods where the initial density of seedlings may be even greater than in plantations. However in a natural wood the dying trees fall to enrich the soil and provide food for beetles and fungi. Also, with natural thinning, different species and numbers survive in different parts of the wood. Here voles kill off the young limes allowing ash to grow on, there the beech suffer from a drought while oak thrives, elsewhere lime and beech gradually grow above the oak and ash and shade them out. Furthermore the results of natural thinning are unlikely to be the same from one time to the next, even on the same spot. Thus is the individuality of semi-natural woods produced and maintained. There is no set pattern such as is in

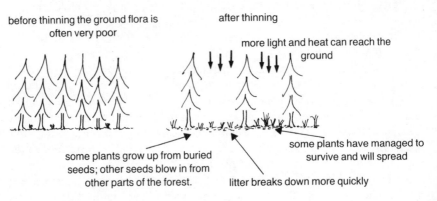

before thinning the ground flora is often very poor

after thinning

more light and heat can reach the ground

some plants grow up from buried seeds; other seeds blow in from other parts of the forest.

litter breaks down more quickly

some plants have managed to survive and will spread

Effects of thinning a coniferous plantation.

the mind of the forester when he or she sets to work on a plantation, usually to try to produce a uniform end crop of trees.

The forester's thinning, while it differs from what happens in a natural wood, is nevertheless very important for the wildlife of a plantation. More light and warmth reach the ground through the gaps created in the canopy where the trees are removed. The litter layer starts to break down more quickly releasing nutrients back into the soil. The last feeble-leaved bracken plants that survived the dark thicket can grow now more vigorously and start to spread; other plants like willowherbs appear from seed blown in from the rides. Species reappear from seeds that have been lying dormant in the soil. Some shrubs, such as elder, whose seeds are brought in by birds start to form an understorey. As the variety of plant life in the thinned area builds up again so too does the number and abundance of animals. Bank voles that like some cover at ground level can move back in to the stand; developing bramble thickets may provide nest sites for blackbirds.

The age at which a plantation is first thinned depends on how fast it is growing, the local conditions and whether the thinnings can be sold, but is often between 15 and 30 years. However 5 to 10 years later most of the gaps created by the first thinning have closed over and the process must be repeated if the best trees are to keep growing rapidly. Much the same applies if we are concerned with the response of the plants and animals of the woodland floor. The more frequently thinning occurs and the more trees are removed with each thinning the greater the proportion of the ground that regains and retains a cover of vegetation.

However, not all the species that disappear during the dark thicket stage can take advantage of the more favourable conditions in older thinned plantations; some have seeds that cannot survive more than a year or two buried in the soil and so cannot last through the thicket stage; others have large seeds that need ants to move them from one part of a wood to another, so their spread back into old plantations from which they have been lost is very slow. We do not know how long it might take them to recolonize old plantations fully because in most woods this is the first time trees have ever been grown in this way on the site.

Once a broadleaved wood has been converted to conifers it is likely to remain coniferous, because at the end of the rotation, when the crop is felled, yet more conifers are likely to be planted. There is little evidence to suggest that a second crop of pure conifers in woods that were formerly of broadleaved trees is much richer than the first and there may be a further slow decline of the more sensitive woodland species. For example, suppose the recovery of these species under the mature conifer crop is only to three-quarters the strength of their previous recovery under mature broadleaves, then within three generations, despite this apparently good recovery, the population will have been halved, because each new conifer crop starts from a reduced baseline.

More of our native wildlife may survive where a mixture of conifers and broadleaves has been planted in a wood that was formerly broadleaved. On some estates there are old broadleaved plantations rich in plants and animals that were believed to have been planted as mixtures with conifers in this way in

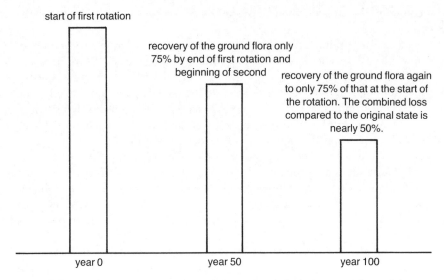

start of first rotation

recovery of the ground flora only
75% by end of first rotation and
beginning of second

recovery of the ground flora again
to only 75% of that at the start of
the rotation. The combined loss
compared to the original state is
nearly 50%.

year 0   year 50   year 100

Effects of successive rotations if recovery and spread of species is only partial.

the nineteenth century. Unfortunately we must be cautious in interpreting the results from such past plantings as a guide to what will happen in woods planted as mixtures now.

Such rich old plantations are the exceptions; perhaps they are the ones where the conifers died or grew poorly, as still happens on some sites today. Also there were no herbicides used when trees were planted in the nineteenth century; finally the countryside was generally richer in wildlife, so that there was more chance than now for species to spread back in when the stands were thinned from nearby woods and hedges. It will be well into the next century before the success of the mixtures planted in the 1940s and '50s is known. We should not risk further losses of plants and animals from ancient woods that have so far escaped large-scale replanting.

Few people have studied what happens in the oakwoods in Wales or the native pinewoods in Scotland when these are replanted with spruce or other introduced conifers, although this has been as widespread as replanting in lowland mixed coppices. Changes to the soils in these woods might be expected to be less significant, since they are generally quite acid already. Many of the herbs and grasses found in these woods (but not all) are well able to recolonize areas at the end of the thicket stage. However the loss of the native tree cover must mean a decline in its associated insects. The characteristic mosses, liverworts and lichens found in these woods are not likely to return in commercial conifer plantations and the communities of the bogs and wet patches found in woods throughout the north and west seldom survive the drainage that occurs when the trees are planted.

A bonus for butterflies?

Botanists have bemoaned the loss of the ground flora in replanted woods, but entomologists have discovered that these are some of the best woods for butterflies at present. The explanation of this apparent paradox is that many butterflies need large open sunny areas. In these grow the plants on which the caterpillars feed as well as plenty of flowers such as thistles, cow parsley, meadowsweet and scabious, from which the adults can take nectar. When coppices were cut regularly such conditions were provided in abundance, but as coppicing declined so the neglected woods became shady throughout and such flowery glades were lost. Many butterflies declined even on some nature reserves and one of the few that increased was the white admiral which likes more shady woods. Now that we know how important open space is in woods, there is much more emphasis on cutting the coppice or creating open glades in other ways.

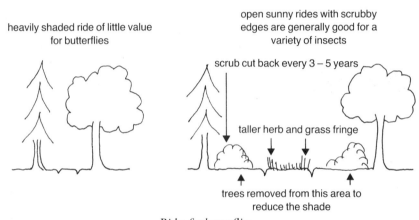

Rides for butterflies.

During the '60s and '70s, however, about the only places where lots of open ground was being created were in ancient woods that were being replanted. The large expanses of open woodland in newly planted areas provided a timely alternative to fresh-cut coppice as a habitat for many animals, but only for a while. As the trees grew and closed canopy so conditions deteriorated for butterflies and the like. Unlike in a worked coppice no new areas would be due for cutting for at least thirty years in most plantations. For some species a second refuge was found in the wide rides created in some commercial forests, particularly where native broadleaved trees and shrubs survived as a fringe.

Such rides and their edges must now be carefully treated if they are to remain suitable for a range of butterflies. Otherwise, for example, rank tall grasses overshade the violets on which the fritillaries feed. Different ways of cutting the grass and shrubby edges have been devised to try to make sure there is always somewhere suitable for the various butterfly species to lay their eggs. Other insects that thrive in the open, sunny woodland favoured by many of our butterflies also benefit from this ride management.

Such systems add to the costs of running the plantation, but take only a fraction of the total area under the tree crop. Thus many foresters have adopted them enthusiastically, as one of the most cost-effective ways of improving plantations for conservation. We do not know how successful ride management alone will be in the long term as a means of preserving butterfly (and other insect) populations. The concentration of open glade species into just a small part of the wood increases the risks that they may be wiped out if the management is altered in one year or the weather is particularly unfavourable.

Where are the beetles?

An abundance of butterflies indicates that conditions are right for the insects that thrive in the young open stages of the woodland cycle, but equally scarce nationally are the flies and beetles that feed on dead and dying wood. Many of these were not well served by coppice management, but did survive in pollarded trees on the boundaries of the wood or in big, partially rotten coppice stools. Changing the wood so that the trees grow as high forest, even in plantations, might allow these specialists in decay more scope to thrive, but in practice the trees are harvested while they are still very young. Spruces, pines and larches that could grow for 200 years if left alone are cut when they are 50 or 60 years; oaks are cut at 100 to 120 years when they have barely left their youth. Also, many of the species that feed on broadleaved timber cannot live in conifers.

Commercial foresters have viewed an abundance of dead trees and branches with understandable concern. For them such trees represent a loss of income from wood that could otherwise have been sold and a threat to the value of what remains. If a dead branch allows rot into the heart of the tree then what could have been worth several hundred pounds for oak veneer or high quality planking becomes little more than firewood. There may also be some risk of pests and diseases spreading from dead and dying trees to the live ones and killing them, although this last is seldom a problem with broadleaved trees.

As yet there has been no apparent benefit for the species that live in really old trees and dead wood from the conversion of coppice woods to plantations, even where plantations of broadleaved trees have been created. Furthermore the old coppice stools and boundary pollards that did provide some habitat for these species have usually been removed during the replanting. However, just as well managed rides can help the butterflies survive in replanted woods so there may be a chance for more beetles, flies and fungi in future if four or five broadleaved trees (or pines in the native pinewoods) were left through every hectare to grow to magnificent old age and bountiful decay.

Birds and mammals

Many birds and mammals become less abundant in ancient woods when they have been replanted with conifers because there is less cover for them where the ground flora or shrub layers are sparse, or because their food – plants or animals – have declined. Dormice, for example, become less common because they do not like to cross the large open spaces found in young plantations and even when the plantation gets old it usually lacks a shrub layer to provide the aerial paths that these animals need. Only where there is much broadleaved regrowth among the plantation are they likely to thrive. Similarly, capercaillie seem to require a small-scale mosaic of old pines in among open ground and young scrubby patches which are seldom found even in pine plantations. However, most birds and mammals range quite widely through a wood. In one study willow warblers concentrated their feeding and nesting in any unplanted patches or remnants of the former woodland cover that were left on the edges of a replanted area, but still made some use of the plantations when they were suitable. Thus they have been able to adapt to plantations better than many invertebrates which feed in much more restricted areas and are less able to move from one patch to the next.

Some conifers in a broadleaved wood may be valuable winter cover and shelter for birds when most of our native trees are leafless. Bird and bat boxes have been installed in plantations to make up for the lack of old trees with holes for nest or roost sites. Such boxes do not replace the need for old trees for species like woodpeckers that feed on the insects within rotten wood, but they are a worthwhile conservation measure.

Plantations of the future

Concern about the losses of wildlife caused by the replanting of ancient woods became widespread in the early '80s as part of a wider public reaction against the replacement of broadleaved trees by conifers. The Forestry Commission was asked to review its (and hence effectively the government's) policies on broadleaved woods. The results were in some respects revolutionary. In future the presumption would be against the clearance of broadleaved woodland for farming or other purposes; broadleaved woods should remain broadleaved; special treatment would be accorded to ancient semi-natural woods to ensure that their special character was maintained. Felling and replanting would still be allowed, but guidelines were produced to go with the new policy. These were meant to help avoid the more drastic changes brought about previously under regimes where efficient timber production was the main guiding force.

Shortly after the review of broadleaves policy a similar exercise was carried out to look at how the treatment of the ancient native pinewoods under forestry schemes might be improved. As with ancient broadleaved woods, some of these had been replanted with introduced conifers such as spruce, with a loss of their characteristic structure and wildlife. The changes in policy proposed for the pinewoods following that review have much in common with those proposed for broadleaves. However, a step forward has been taken in that there are now specific recommendations to avoid draining wet, boggy areas which form an integral part of the pinewood system and to encourage natural regeneration and the planting of seeds from locally grown trees.

An innovation, which more or less coincided with these policy changes, and which certainly made the promotion of broadleaves easier, was the development of the tree shelter. These are the round or square plastic tubes that appear to have sprouted in field corners all over the country. Sometimes they look like an untidy graveyard, but they speed up the growth of most broadleaved trees and give the saplings some protection from rabbits and small deer. They have made it much cheaper to plant small blocks than when every area had to be fenced. Fewer trees need be planted to fill a gap because their growth and survival in the first few years is so much greater. The trees can also be planted in irregular patterns since the tubes are easy to spot when it is time to weed round the trees. Once the tree has grown out of the tube and the plastic has disintegrated (they are meant to degrade under the influence of ultra-violet light) the result may be a more natural-looking plantation.

It is clear that the broadleaves policy has been a great step forward; it is less common for owners to apply either for complete clearance of ancient woods or for wholesale conversion of broadleaved woods to conifers. However there are still schemes where the scale of felling causes concern, with perhaps 2-3 hectares in a 6-hectare wood proposed for clear-felling at one time. Owners and foresters are often still keen to include some fast-growing conifers or introduced broadleaved species in planting schemes, rather than sticking to the species strictly native to the site; and the use of coppice and natural regeneration instead of planting have not been adopted as much as would be desirable from a nature conservation point of view. On the other hand, there is much more interest in using trees from the locality in planting schemes in pinewoods, there is less draining of boggy patches within woods and less insistence on planting 100 per cent of the available ground.

Nevertheless, while clear-felling and replanting remain the predominant methods in British forestry, there is still a long way to go.

Reversing the conifer tide

It is a measure of how much attitudes have changed in the last decade that conifers planted in old broadleaved sites in the '50s and '60s are being removed to try and reverse the damage that had been done by their planting in the first place.

Despite good intentions and support from public funds, the conifers planted on many ancient sites from 1945 onwards did not thrive. This was particularly so in woods on the heavy clays of the Midlands. Regrowth from coppice stumps swamped the planted trees which had much smaller root systems and so were more prone to drought or water-logging. Sometimes the spruce and pine can still be found in these woods as spindly individuals amongst young ash poles; in some places they have disappeared altogether. The opportunity exists to try to make the most of the new broadleaved crop rather than attempting to rescue the conifers.

This is happening in woods sold off by the Forestry Commission and bought by local wildlife trusts, for example at Tiddesley Wood just outside Pershore in Worcestershire. Elsewhere the Forestry Commission themselves have taken the lead. They have recognized that nature conservation needs may outweigh

Two Spruce in Place of One Oak

before restoration

1 – 2 species per 25 m² in the ground flora covering only about 5% of the ground

after restoration

8 – 10 species per 25m²

40 – 50% ground cover

Taking out the conifers at Dalavich.

commercial considerations in these ancient woods. They are restoring the northern part of Chalkney Wood in Essex, to a small-leaved lime mixture similar to that which survives in the southern portion managed by Essex County Council. Brooding hulks of oak at Sherwood Forest have been freed from a crowd of young conifers. Spruce and even introduced strains of Scots pine are being cut out of the native pinewoods at Glenmore.

One of the most dramatic changes has been at Dalavich Oakwood on the shores of Loch Awe. This was planted with dense fir and spruce in the late '50s and where the conifers remain it is difficult to appreciate that many oaks were left among the plantings. Where, however, these planted trees have been cut out, the oakwood reappears. We do not know how long it will take for all the typical oakwood plants and animals to return. Some have come back very quickly, others are spreading more slowly and for some the conditions that they require may no longer exist. Dalavich contained many wet hollows that were drained and may never recover their original composition. Not all that has been lost can be restored, but ancient woods have proved more resilient than we dared hope fifteen years ago.

The first priority in woodland conservation must be to stop converting more ancient semi-natural woodland into large-scale even-aged plantations using introduced species. What should then be done with the many ancient woods, particularly the large woods, that have been replanted with conifers with great loss to our native woodland communities? Something can be salvaged by good ride management, by encouraging native trees and shrubs, by creating as much variety in the structure of their woods as possible. Without this reversal there is likely to be a progressive loss of the rarer and more interesting species in each future rotation at the thicket stage; the butterflies and other species of open ground for which some plantations are currently excellent will also be lost.

We could, however, do more: some plantations could be put back completely to native trees and shrubs to regain much of their former glory – if foresters could be encouraged to follow the examples set at Chalkney and Dalavich Woods.

However, even if all the plantations in ancient woods could be transformed back to something like a semi-natural state they would still cover only about 2 per cent of the country. So we must look also at the prospects for wildlife in the woods that have naturally grown up in the last few hundred years, which may provide opportunities for linking up ancient woods and allowing more chance for their special wildlife to spread out.

5

Woods that Grow while Our Backs are Turned

In the eastern states of America the woodland cover has gone from about 10 per cent to 80 per cent in the last hundred years. Scattered through these forests are the abandoned walls and ruins of farms left as the people moved to more fertile ground further west. With no interference much of our own country would return to woodland, as has happened in America. Ash seedlings abound in my garden, and among the heather in the Orkneys birch is spreading out from the most northerly natural woodland in Britain.

Each autumn winged seeds of birch blow on to open moorland; fruits of blackthorn and hawthorn are eaten by birds and their seed deposited in fields. Jays bury thousands of individual acorns and while they do find and dig up most of them during the winter, inevitably some are missed. Every year some seeds grow into seedlings, only to die because the moor is burnt or the field grazed.

Occasionally conditions are right for one or two, or perhaps a whole host, of these seeds not only to develop into seedlings but then to grow into young trees. This happened in the '50s when rabbits almost died out because of myxomatosis. Suddenly commons and bits of downland sprouted shrubs and young trees, now well-developed woodland. Along many railway lines the railway fences gave some protection from grazing to tree seedlings and when steam trains gave way to diesel, and the railway banks were no longer burnt, these seedlings grew away. Now strips of young birch are a common feature by the track. Peat bogs in the north and west should be too wet to support trees, but as the great raised mires of Lancashire and Cumbria were cut away and drained, so woods of birch and pine develop on what was left.

New woods also spring up whenever farming is in the doldrums, usually on the poorest land or land which is difficult to farm for other reasons. Such woods may not last long and may be cleared once the pressure for land increases again. Throughout Deeside the birchwoods have played musical chairs since 1945. The total area is about the same now as then, but about half the woods present in 1945 have gone, while a similar area has appeared in other places.

Back on the edges, and even in the centre of towns and cities, trees and shrubs sneak into old quarries, derelict land and closed up cemeteries. New woods creep along the miles of railways axed after the Beeching report in the '60s and the verges of new motorways are also scrubbing over.

Scrub and recent woods

If an area is left free from grazing and burning for a while, a few trees or shrubs may get started. Islands of scrub form. The trees and bushes themselves eventually produce more seed and also attract birds who inadvertently bring in seeds of other species. If conditions change again, for example, grazing increases or there is a fire, then these patches of scrub just stay the same size or even decrease. Many of the hawthorns scattered through fields in north Wales are all about the same age. They are the survivors from such an invasion of the fields that was not sustained.

Sometimes scrub growth continues. The patches with their skirts of bramble or bracken grow and fuse, a closed canopy of trees and shrubs forms and there is a new piece of woodland. The changes do not stop at this point however.

Under young birch on moor or heath, the heather may first be replaced by bilberry, then by grasses. These are better able to grow under the shade and are more suited to the changes that are taking place in the soil under birch which becomes richer and less acid than under heather. The mats of grass and the shade stop further birch regeneration for a while. Eventually however trees die and gaps are made in the canopy. The trees may blow over so that bare soil is exposed. The conditions are now right to allow in more birch seedlings, with perhaps also some pine or oak, rowan or hazel if these are in the vicinity.

Under the dense thorn thickets that develop on old lowland fields almost all plants other than a few mosses disappear for a time. Some of these thickets remain more or less the same for decades. Others shelter oak and ash saplings from grazing and these eventually over-top their protectors. Holly, bramble, gorse and juniper may similarly protect young trees that establish in their midst. The thorns and holly can usually survive under the shade of oak and ash but many of the junipers that once grew at Kingley Vale (Sussex) have died out. Their skeletons can be found under the dark yews that grew up with them.

Ancient semi-natural woods have had much the same composition for often hundreds, if not thousands of years. It is a characteristic of more recent woods that they are changing; at Holme Fen, Cambridgeshire, for example, is a birch wood that has grown up on the site of Whittlesey Mere which was drained in the nineteenth century. Now there are oaks among the birch and what is now one of the largest birchwoods in England may be an oakwood in a hundred years' time.

During the early stages of woodland formation the range of plants and animals present may be very wide. There are those that live in the open ground but also those that use the developing scrub, including many woodland edge species. In southern Britain shrubs with attractive flowers and berries are common at this stage and attract many insects and birds.

NUMBERS OF INSECTS ASSOCIATED WITH DIFFERENT SHRUBS

Hawthorn	230	Whitebeams	36
Blackthorn	157	Buckthorn	27
Crab apple	133	Spindle	19
Hazel	107	Elder	19
Rose	107	Dogwood	18
Bramble	107	Clematis	18
Gorse	52	Viburnums	17
Honeysuckle	48	Yew	6
Field maple	41	Box	4

Once the canopy has closed the species of old meadow or heath are lost. It is then largely a question of waiting for the species of ancient woodland to come in and spread – which may take decades or centuries. In Hayley Wood in Cambridgeshire, oxlips have only crept a few metres into an adjacent piece of woodland that has grown up on old fields since 1922. Dog's mercury shows a similar rate of spread from a hedge into the Geesetoft Wilderness (Hertfordshire) which has grown up on land left uncultivated for about a hundred years. Sometimes plants like sanicle seem to occur in lines along paths perhaps from seeds brought in on the legs of deer or on the clothes of visiting botanists.

Birds and mammals can spread more easily than plants into new woods and are particularly attracted to those that have a varied tree and shrub layer. Thus even young woods may have nesting blackbirds and robins, bank voles and hedgehogs. Indeed many nineteenth-century spinneys (hawthorn and black-thorn clumps), now grown into tall woodland, were first encouraged as fox coverts or for pheasant cover.

How to identify a recent wood

A glance at an old map may tell you which woods are recent, because they will not be shown! If you can't find an old map, look at the wood itself: there may be signs that the ground was once ploughed, with evidence of the old ridges and furrows that in some cases are remnants of medieval strip farming. This is often best looked for in winter when the ground flora is scarce. The low-lying furrows can sometimes be picked out because they hold water or snow longer than the adjacent ridge. There may be the remains of old field boundaries (walls, hedges or fences depending on where you are) or even farm buildings among the trees as in the abandoned land in America. Recent woods do sometimes contain big old trees, perhaps from an old hedgerow that has been swallowed up, but more usually most of the trees are young and fairly even-aged. Unlike in ancient woods, coppice stools are rare. These woods have mostly been born of neglect and few have been around long enough for their timber to be worth cutting.

Pioneer trees that can invade open ground, such as birch, pine and oak, or ash on richer soils, are common. Thorns and elder, rather than hazel, are the typical shrubs present, with sallows in wet areas and buddleia in urban ones. There is no absolute rule. Beechwoods have formed on the acid sands and gravels of south Buckinghamshire, birch and pine invade heaths in Surrey and Hampshire, oak comes up on Essex commons. In Deeside old fields may become covered by juniper, as they do in Scandinavia; the impounded area created in 1816 at Loch Fleet is now a magnificent wood of alder and willows. Sycamore moves in quickly to many a derelict site in towns and cities, while the nineteenth-century landslip between Axmouth and Lyme Regis has an even more exotic touch with large stands of the Mediterranean holm oak.

Gaps in the wood tend to contain the plants of the rough grassland or heath on which the wood has grown, rather than the woodland edge plants found in gaps in ancient woods. Under the canopy there may be few plants typical of woodland because there has been little time for the more demanding species to spread in.

The lack of 'ancient woodland indicators' (see chapter 3) amongst the plants and animals in a wood can sometimes be used (with caution) as a sign that a wood is probably recent. Plants and animals, however, are no respecters of ecologist's theories and on Wytham Hill near Oxford they spread much more quickly, perhaps because of the light limestone soil, perhaps because of the way that ancient and modern woods are so intricately mixed there. Several species now grow in what was an arable field until six years ago and only herb Paris seems to have stuck fairly closely within the ancient woodland boundary banks.

Often just a few species predominate over most of the ground. Many recent woods have a ground carpet of ivy whereas in ancient woods this is unusual except in the west. Banks of nettles pick out patches that are particularly high in phosphates, perhaps the site of an old building or rubbish tip. Brambles sprawl everywhere. In the less shaded areas grasses such as Yorkshire fog and false oat-grass cover the floor and cow parsley provides a lacey edge to the wood. On acid soils in the west, where it is wetter, there are fewer differences between ancient and recent woods, at least as far as herbs and grasses are concerned. Bluebells and primroses grow on open sea-cliffs and along hedges, so that it is not surprising that they can also be found in new woods. There is however usually a greater variety of mosses, liverworts and lichens in ancient woods compared to recent woods even in the west.

Management of recent semi-natural woodland

Recent woodland and scrub can be managed for wildlife in much the same way as ancient woods. In general, native trees and shrubs and a varied woodland structure should be encouraged. There is however less justification in recent woods for seeking to eliminate all alien species than in ancient sites where the special flora and fauna have developed over hundreds of years. Those of recent woods are inevitably changing and provide a test bed for finding out which new combinations of species will survive in future.

Some recent woods have been coppiced, but then the stools are usually small because they have been cut only a few times compared to those in ancient coppice woods. There are likely to be fewer species that depend on the coppice cycle to survive and so there is less reason to promote coppicing in recent woods, unless it fits with the other uses for the site. For example, the wood might be being managed to provide firewood, in which case coppicing could meet both this and wildlife needs.

More commonly recent woods have a high forest structure. The trees are often tall and crowded, casting a dense shade, since it is unlikely that they have ever been thinned. The priority from a nature conservation point of view then depends on how old the trees are and how long they have been neglected. Usually the best thing to do is to create some open space, to thin the wood if possible and let the light get to the woodland floor as in a plantation. Not only will the wildlife benefit but the owner can harvest some timber. However if the wood has not been managed at all for a very long time, perhaps for more than a century, its structure may be moving towards that of a wildwood. If possible, it should be allowed to continue in this natural development.

Young woodland and scrub that have not completely closed canopy present the manager with a different set of options. The mixture of patchy open scrub or trees and grassland or heath is often very species-rich and worth retaining in this form. Usually this means cutting back the scrub from time to time. At Castor Hanglands, a nature reserve near Peterborough, some of the scrub is cut on a cyclical basis so that parts of it are always young and open.

Hedgerows

Recent woods and scrub often have many of the same species as hedgerows. While some hedgerows are as old as the ancient woods that they connect, others come from post-1600 enclosures. The latter tend to have only one or two shrub or tree species in them, whereas hedges that have been carved out of the woods during land clearance have a wider range of species. Thus the mixture of oak, hornbeam, hazel and elm in the eastern part of Plegdon Wood (Essex) can still be seen in the hedge that was left on the edge of the field when the woodland was cleared. In some parts of the country the number of trees and shrubs in a hedge may indicate just how old it is: the greater the variety, the older the hedge. This does not always work, because some hedges were planted as mixtures, and the further north you are the fewer species there are available to go into the hedge, but it gives a rough guide.

The plants along a hedge base may be rather dull, because they get treated with herbicides or receive some of the fertilizer applied to the field which encourages a small range of vigorous species such as cleavers and sterile brome grass. However some old hedges may have woodland herbs and grasses along

the remnant half of Plegdon Wood

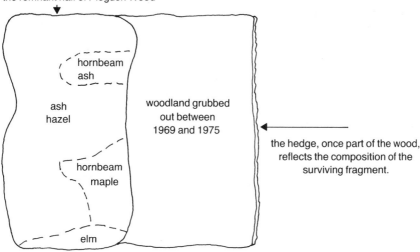

Ghost hedges at Plegdon. Some hedges once formed part of a wood that has since been cleared. As here, they may retain the mixture of species that were present in the wood.

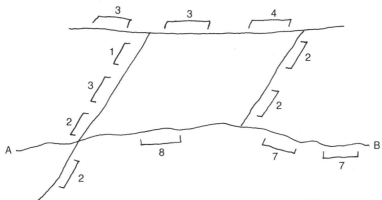

Hedgerow dating: count the number of tree and shrub species in a 30 m section; repeat to get several samples and take the average. (In the diagram numbers represent number of species present in a 30m section.) Very roughly each extra species suggest an extra 100 years on the hedge age.

Hedge A to B appears to derive from the early medieval period (mean no. trees and shrubs 7.3), whereas the others are probably enclosure hedges only 2 – 300 years old.

their bases, such as dog's mercury, bluebells and primroses. These could be survivors from when the hedge was part of a wood, but others may have gradually spread along them from nearby woods. The reverse also happens – plants from old hedges may colonize new woodland nearby. Woodland birds and small mammals live in hedges as well as using them as corridors to get from one wood to another. Hedgerows, it is reckoned, contain about 90 million trees, so that as well as providing links between woods hedges are important for wildlife in their own right.

The grubbing out of hedges and the losses of large elms to Dutch elm disease were issues that helped to increase public awareness of the countryside changes and the conservation of wildlife during the 1970s and '80s. Hedgerows are still being lost but there are now proposals that they should be protected – as trees can be – by preservation orders.

New hedges are being planted. While these do not compensate for the loss of an old one, they will help a bit. There is also a revival of interest in the restoration of hedge management by coppicing and laying. New hedgerow trees are being planted, or, better still, self-sown saplings tagged so that they will not be cut when the hedge is next trimmed. Even Dutch Elm disease may now be waning. Big old elms will remain a rarity for many years but there are many places where there is vigorous regrowth of small elm poles along the hedges. If this is kept relatively low and young by cutting there is hope that elm will survive and thrive into the twenty-first century, because it seems that the beetle that spreads the disease prefers to feed in larger trees.

A role for recent semi-natural woods?

Recent semi-natural woods and scrub are among the least studied woodland in Britain. They are often on the fringes of areas that are valued for other reasons, for example grassland sites, so that recent woods are often the ones that nature conservationists are trying hardest to remove! Many people who go out with the British Trust for Conservation Volunteers, or join a work party on a local nature reserve, find themselves 'scrub-bashing'. That's the name affectionately given to the clearing of trees and shrubs where they have invaded old grassland or heath. This is necessary to maintain these rich open communities with their distinctive plants and animals, but it can lead to the impression that all scrub and recent woodland is of little value for wildlife. This is not true and fortunately those who have attempted such tasks know too well the resilience of the trees and shrubs.

Recent woods have great potential for wildlife and they are the best way to add to the existing woodland cover from a nature conservation point of view. If areas around ancient woods and along corridors connecting woods could be left to scrub up and naturally develop into woodland, the existing woods would be buffered against change; the new woods would be richer than if developed in isolation and species would have more chance to spread from one site to another. Such corridors may become very important if changes occur in our climate. Our countryside would also become more diverse. Many places could be livened up by a bit of scrub without interfering with ancient rich grassland or heath. In particular natural regeneration of scrub and woodland can be used to add variety to what is now the most common type of woodland in Britain – plantations on open ground.

6

Tree Farming or Bold New Landscapes?

Joseph of Arimathea should perhaps be the patron saint of British foresters. He stuck his staff into the ground in Somerset and it became the Glastonbury thorn – but I doubt if he was the first to plant trees in Britain. Planting fruit trees to form orchards probably preceded establishment of trees for timber, and in the twelfth and thirteenth centuries there were laws in Wales which gave special value to trees planted for ornament and shelter.

Now planting trees on open ground is so common that most of our forests have been formed in this way, and it is the image that most commonly occurs when British forestry is mentioned. The consequences of this for the structure and composition of woods and hence for their wildlife are considerable. Some species have increased and spread, others have declined. What is certain is that we are not recreating the same type of forest as once covered the hills. Instead a new landscape and new wildlife habitats are emerging.

Plantations for pleasure and profit

Planting trees on a large scale became popular in the eighteenth and nineteenth century, stimulated by the earlier writings of John Evelyn and new ideas on landscape and sport. The view from the big house might be paramount in the location of particular specimen trees and the shape of the woods in the parkland; the arrangement of the rides would be influenced by the owner's tastes in sport and recreation; but the value of the timber that would come from these plantations was also very much appreciated. New plantings expanded rather quicker in Scotland than in the rest of Britain. Tree nurseries developed and many seedlings and saplings were transported from Scotland to estates elsewhere. This might involve taking them by sea round the coast and then carting them inland to their final destination, often some way from the coast.

Trees brought from Europe (European larch, Norway spruce and silver fir) and from North America (Sitka spruce, Weymouth pine, Douglas fir) were planted with varying success. Several species grew to large sizes, producing straight, even-grained timber, much more quickly than most of our native trees, particularly in the mild, moist west. Such timber suited the changing industrial methods in which wood was easily trimmed to the thickness required; previously the time needed to saw up timber by hand meant that it was generally easier to work with whole small trees which were cut when they had reached the right size for the job. The quality of the wood fibre for paper-making was becoming increasingly important and spruces are particularly valuable in this respect. The experience gained by these pioneering planters proved invaluable when the Forestry Commission began its afforestation programme in the twentieth century.

Not that all planting was with trees from abroad. At Cawdor there is a two-hundred-year-old plantation of Scots pine established on open moor that is now full of the pinewood orchid, creeping lady's tresses. Oak was planted widely on many of the richer soils and more sheltered ground, particularly in the Welsh Borders. Often the oak was established in mixtures with larch or spruce. Beech was found to grow well in northern England and in Scotland, and used well beyond its native range. As an example of what was being done, the Duke of Argyll in 1832 had 55,000 oaks, 12,000 larch, 18,000 Scots pine and 10,000 spruce put in on his lands around Inverary.

Some trees soon fell out of favour. Weymouth pine was attacked by blister rust, a fungus disease also found on currants. Some of the early plantings of European larch used seed collected from high mountain areas in central Europe. These did not grow well in our milder, but more unpredictable climate, because they were very susceptible to damage by late frosts. Later, seed was collected from areas where the climate is more like ours and better results were obtained. Moreover a chance planting of European larch next to the closely related species, Japanese larch, produced a hybrid that grew even better than did its parents.

The expansion of large-scale plantations

In the early part of this century the Manchester Water Company started planting in the Thirlmere catchment in the Lake District. These plantations were a pointer to what was to follow, not just in upland Britain, but on many poor soils in the lowlands. The grass and heath of the old Breckland landscape around Thetford were planted in the '20s and '30s by the Forestry Commission. Huge forests were created on the shifting sands of Culbin near Nairn and on the dunes at Newborough on Anglesey, rather as the French planted up large areas with maritime pine in the Les Landes region. Other forests appeared around the fringes of the Lake District, in North Wales and southern Scotland. At Kielder in Northumberland some 50,000 hectares were planted in just one block over about twenty years.

The location of these new plantations was as much influenced by changing agricultural fortunes as had been the clearance of the wildwood and the survival of ancient woodland elsewhere. The Forestry Commission was told to create a strategic timber reserve as quickly as possible; as it had little money with which to do it, it needed cheap land, land of less value to agriculture. There were also plans that forestry should provide an alternative form of rural employment in depressed areas, which again pointed to parts of the country where farming was least profitable. There is relatively little poor quality farmland in the lowlands; what there is exists in fairly small parcels of woods, meadows and wetlands. These were not suitable for the big planting schemes needed if the Forestry Commission was to meet its targets.

Inevitably, therefore, the biggest growth in commercial forestry took place in the uplands of north and west Britain. Whereas formerly the south-east was the most wooded area, now the balance of Britain's woodland cover has shifted towards the north-west, first through the work of the Forestry Commission, more recently through that of private land owners and forestry companies. The transfer of the Forestry Commission's headquarters from London to Edinburgh reflects this trend.

Land of low farming value is generally of high wildlife value and provides the only large-scale wild, open landscape that we have. Hence there was a considerable outcry when such scenery and the plants and animals it contains were perceived to be under threat from forestry. Not that forestry has been the only cause of damaging changes in the hills. Heather has disappeared from many moors as a result of too many sheep now being kept. Nevertheless the conflict of interests between forestry and conservation has often been stark and bitter. Elsewhere there are arguments against the planting of lodgepole pine in parts of Scandinavia and of eucalyptus in southern Europe. So it is not a peculiarly British phenomenon.

The wildlife of new upland plantations

Almost from the outset the large new plantings of the Forestry Commission were criticized for their sombre appearance. An early broadside was launched against a proposal to plant up part of the southern Lake District. H. H. Symonds wrote 'where there was colour, this is first hidden, then dissolved: grasses, moss, plant-life perish as the trees form a canopy . . . What is seen is the rigid and monotonous ranks of spruce, dark green to blackish, goose-stepping on the fell side.'

It would have been naive to imagine that what the Director-General of the Forestry Commission described in 1980 as 'the most thorough alteration to the pattern of life on UK hillsides since clearance of the ancient forests' would not lead to changes in the wildlife of the hills also. As our appreciation of the international importance of some of the species and communities found in the uplands increased, so did the level of criticism of modern forestry. Unfortunately, although modern forestry has been in existence for about a century, it is only in the last decade or so that foresters generally have come to take nature conservation very seriously.

There is now more understanding of what may be lost and a greater willingness to try to locate new forests in less sensitive areas, but it is not possible to avoid changes when an open landscape is converted into a forested one.

The plants of wet ground and in particular of mires and deep peat are currently the most seriously threatened by afforestation. Most cannot survive under shade and the drainage that goes with planting can completely destroy the structure of these communities even in the small patches left unplanted in the forest. Careless ploughing and drainage may also damage mires adjacent to the new forest. The plants of dry moorland are more likely to be able to survive within the forest in open rides and glades, but again there are few that can live under the trees, so they become much less common.

Many birds of open heath, bog or moor are similarly at a disadvantage as bog pools disappear and the trees start to grow. This has been a major argument against the rapid expansion of forestry, particularly recently in the northern peatlands of Caithness and Sutherland. Some of the birds that are displaced when an area is planted, for example the skylark, may be relatively common, but others such as greenshank are rare.

There have been significant reductions in the populations of upland birds including curlew, golden plover, dunlin, snipe and greenshank which have been caused in part by the expansion of forestry. The dense mass of large-scale afforestation breaks up the feeding range of birds of prey such as golden eagle. Less live prey or carrion is available to them and they may rear fewer young in consequence or abandon those territories altogether.

What is lost differs from one region to another and changes due to forestry may be mixed up with changes in how the sheep on the hill are farmed or grouse moors managed. The precise effects of new afforestation on upland wildlife are still the subject of much research. There are parts of the uplands where any adverse effects of commercial forestry could be minimized by better forest design or by planting on only a small scale. Large-scale schemes should not be ruled out completely, though, because there may be areas where they would be acceptable.

However, regardless of what new planting comes along there are already big plantations on the hills which in most cases are likely to stay. What are the species that have spread into them or might appear in them in the future if more care is taken over their management? These plantations cover such vast areas compared with ancient and semi-natural woods that there may be opportunities to make up in part by quantity what they may lack in the quality of their wildlife.

The modern plantation as habitat for wildlife

The majority of recent plantations are composed of conifers, with Sitka spruce being the species most often planted. This is an evergreen and differs from almost all our native trees; yew and juniper are the only evergreen short-needled native conifers and these rarely form groves of more than a few hectares. The predominance of spruce in afforestation schemes is a major reason why new plantations can bear little resemblance to either surviving semi-natural woods or to the wildwood that once covered much of the uplands and the lowland heaths.

Between 1945 and 1980 the drive to plant up as much land as possible inevitably resulted in large even-aged stands so that there is not even much variety in the ages and size of trees at present in many forests. This at least should change in the future. Some areas are being felled early, some retained for longer than usual to break up the age pattern.

Parts of western Britain are so windy that some of these forests cannot be thinned, as would be done in lowland woods, or else large patches of the forest blow down. There is therefore no opportunity to let more light reach the forest floor and so encourage the ground flora or to increase the diversity of the stands by favouring any birch trees that might be struggling away among the spruce. All this makes most recent plantations appear very gloomy; but they are not the wildlife deserts that they have sometimes been called.

Plants of the first rotation

Before the land is planted it usually has to be fenced to keep out deer and sheep which would otherwise eat the young trees. Plants previously kept short by grazing or burning grow tall and lush. The tussocks of grass, heather or bilberry provide food and cover for voles and other small mammals (although these also may gnaw at the trees), attracting predators such as the short-eared owl. Most of this vegetation disappears as the trees grow and the canopy closes.

The plantations are generally on ground that has been unwooded for at least three hundred and often nearer a thousand years. There are few if any woodland plants and animals already there, to spread and take advantage of the new tree cover. These plantations start off therefore in a poorer state (in terms of wildlife) than those established on ancient woodland sites.

On peat soils only a few mosses may survive under the dense shade. In the odd gap where a tree has died, a few ferns, wood sorrel, or wavy-hair grass may show, but because often the trees cannot be thinned or they would blow down, these woodland plants get little chance to spread through the stand as it gets older. Eventually the trees are felled or are blown over and plants of open ground can thrive again. However, much of the life of the crop is spent in the dense thicket stage which is inhospitable for higher plants.

There is more ground cover under trees that have been planted on a richer mineral soil, or in places where they can be thinned, such as at Coed y Brenin in North Wales or in the lowland pine plantations at Thetford (Norfolk). Sometimes there may even be the beginnings of a shrub layer of broadleaved trees. The woodland plants that spread into such stands usually include bramble and bracken. Others often encountered are rosebay, broad buckler-fern and creeping soft-grass. Not only must they be able to colonize woods that are often a long way from any existing tree cover, but also they must be able to tolerate a type of tree cover very different to that found in most semi-natural woods. Hence they tend to be plants that are already common and widespread. Even so there is only a limited period during which there is much of a woodland ground flora before the trees are felled, usually between the ages of 50 and 60 years.

In the clear-felled areas plants spread rapidly among the small twigs and branches and the tops of the trees that are left after harvesting. Few can have survived from previous open ground communities but some, such as creeping soft-grass, that may grow in old plantations, are now able to spread rapidly. Others such as rushes spring up from seed buried in the soil, willow-herb seeds float in from other parts of the forest, while there may also be some invasion from adjacent rides.

What develops is seldom the same as was there before the trees came. The branches and litter left from the tree crop gradually break down and enrich the soil. The soils are disturbed and better drained which does not suit peatland species like the Sphagnum mosses. There is less grazing and no burning of the vegetation so that low growing species like tormentil may not be able to compete with the taller herbs like rosebay and rank tussocky grasses. This new vegetation flourishes for five to ten years before the dense shade returns when the next generation of planted trees closes canopy.

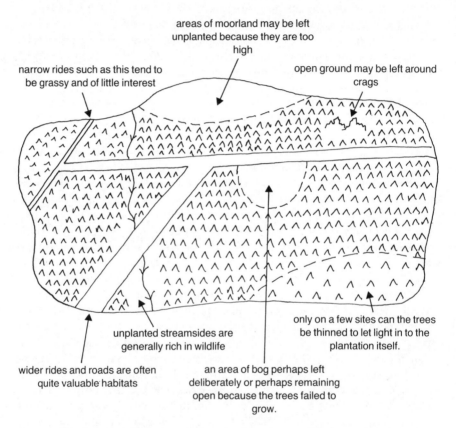

areas of moorland may be left unplanted because they are too high

narrow rides such as this tend to be grassy and of little interest

open ground may be left around crags

unplanted streamsides are generally rich in wildlife

only on a few sites can the trees be thinned to let light in to the plantation itself.

wider rides and roads are often quite valuable habitats

an area of bog perhaps left deliberately or perhaps remaining open because the trees failed to grow.

The importance of open space in new plantations and forms it may take.

Open space and its importance

Because in many upland coniferous forests very few plants can survive under the trees the wildlife found in the 15-20 per cent of the forest that is not planted becomes particularly important. This open ground can often be very varied.

Some of it is made up of the rides and roads needed to work the forest. In some forests there are small riverside meadows left over when the main part of the farm was planted. Then there are grassy areas – 'lawns' – where deer are encouraged to feed, so that they can be easily counted and if necessary shot safely. If such open ground can be mown or grazed then there may be opportunities to recreate in a small way some of the open moorland communities that flourished before the plantations were formed.

Ponds were often created to provide water to help fight forest fires, although they are less important for this now and may be retained largely for the plants, frogs, duck and fish that have moved in. Small quarries are dug to provide stone for forest roads, producing in the process wet rock faces that are favoured locations for the growth of mosses.

Strips of land along the sides of streams were sometimes left unplanted because the ground was too steep to plough. More areas should be left unplanted in future. New guidelines discourage planting on streamsides or on bogs and in some cases trees planted in such situations are being removed.

Many upland areas have remnants of broadleaved woodland in the sheltered valleys. In the past these were often cleared or underplanted with conifers at the same time as the rest of the plantation was established. Now such areas are likely to be retained, partly to help improve the appearance of these new forests in the landscape. If the old woods are brought within the forest fence there may be a chance for them to regenerate and spread, which did not happen when they were part of the grazed moorland. It is important therefore that some open space is left around such woodland relics. They will then have a chance to expand.

Most of the plant communities and species found within these new forests are fairly common, but at Newborough Warren (Anglesey) and at Culbin sands near Nairn particularly rich and interesting plant communities have survived or developed. In Newborough there are orchid-rich wet hollows (including the dune helleborine) between the planted dunes tops; at Culbin areas of lichen-covered shingle with many rare species occur where the soil has proved too poor in nutrients for tree growth. The Culbin plantations are also noted for their birds and the occurrence of wintergreens and creeping lady's tresses, woodland plants often associated with old native pinewoods. At Thetford in Norfolk some of the little annual plants that formerly occurred on the grass-heath of the Breckland reappear when the plantations are felled. These are species that require disturbed ground and were common where rabbit scrapes and burrows broke up the surface mat of vegetation. Such botanical hot spots are however the exceptions and form only a fraction of the total forest estate.

Birds of the first rotation

Most of the species of the open ground are much less common in the new forests, if they occur at all. Hence there has been justifiable concern about the species that are lost following afforestation of moorland or bog. There have however been gains in our birdlife, which have not always been properly recognized.

In some forests the goshawk was re-introduced and now seems to be thriving. It is a bird that likes large areas of forest in which to hunt. Other species to benefit from the creation of large plantations have been redpolls and siskins, which are generally more common on coniferous than broadleaved trees. The continental form of the crossbill, another conifer specialist, has spread through much of the country, although so far the distinctive Scottish species is largely confined to ancient pinewoods.

Gaps formed when trees blow over, rides, streams and areas left unplanted help to break up vast stretches of even-aged forest and to increase the opportunities for different species to establish breeding populations within the plantations. The main variety comes however where there is a mixture of age classes. Thus short-eared owls may hunt in the rough grass before canopy closure, but tawny owls become the main predator within older plantations. Song-birds are abundant in the thicket stage just as they are in young coppice. Most plantations however do not contain over-mature trees so hole-nesting birds are, not surprisingly, scarce. There might be opportunities to remedy this with time if some stands of well thinned conifers could be allowed to grow to their full stature and ruinous decay. In the meantime hole-nesting birds, such as the pied flycatcher, are being encouraged by the provision of nestboxes. More substantial platforms are even being built in a few places to try to make nesting sites for ospreys.

The birds found in clear-fells (areas after felling) generally differ from those that were found on the open ground that preceded the forest. Species of woodland edge and glade are more common than those that prefer completely open ground such as the skylark. Nevertheless there have been notable developments in some lowland forests and those on the richer soils: woodlarks now breed in clear-fells at Thetford; nightjars breed in young stands in the North York Moors and parts of Wales. Both of these are relatively rare species that were formerly associated with dry heath, which may by why the birds have been able to adapt to such changed habitats; there is no clear evidence that birds of wet moorland and bog will regularly find suitable nesting and feeding grounds within clear-fells.

One way that many plantations might be improved for wildlife in future is by encouraging a greater variety of tree species within them. The main crop may remain as spruce or pine for commercial reasons, but birds are more able than most animals to make use of small patches of broadleaves in amongst the conifers. Even just a group of oak or birch may enable the odd individual bird to survive where it would not otherwise do so, and the total effect of such groups, repeated through the thousands of hectares of new plantation, could be substantial. Larger areas of broadleaves, perhaps along a stream, would allow the development of more stable breeding populations. A mixture of trees can also be important because birds use different species at different times of the year.

There are questions still to be answered about the long-term development of these forests. Will the birds presently common in the native pinewoods (crested tit, Scottish crossbill, capercaillie) eventually come to thrive in the new plantations in the second or third rotation? Will these forests become suitable for buzzards and eagles to hunt through as is the case on the Continent? For most commercial plantations the answer is probably no. A higher proportion of Sitka spruce is being planted in the second rotation in many forests than in the first so despite a greater use of broadleaves in small areas the overall species diversity may decline. The risk of trees blowing over will still restrict the amount of thinning that may be done and will mean that much replanting will have to be in large even-aged patches. On the other hand the forests established under the new native pinewood scheme may be richer and become suitable for these birds since, apart from being composed of native pine, they should have a more irregular structure and much more open space within them. It will however be some years before we can know whether such hopes can be fulfilled.

Mammals and reptiles

In North America and continental Europe there are reptiles and amphibians that spend most of their lives in woodland, but no British species are so restricted. On the contrary our rarest reptiles (sand lizard and smooth snake), which are found mainly on the southern heaths in Dorset, have almost certainly been adversely affected as areas have been planted to pine. They do survive at quite high densities in sunny rides and open areas within the forests but their populations overall have been reduced because the total area of such rides is only a fraction of that of the former open heath. The remnant populations within forests are more vulnerable to accidental extinction since they are restricted to small areas.

Small mammals such as voles thrive in the dense tall vegetation that develops when an area is first fenced before planting, but it is a boom and bust situation, since conditions remain suitable only until the trees close canopy. As the ground flora is shaded out and its cover reduced so are the numbers of these animals. They become confined largely to the rides until the next felling occurs.

Some larger mammals have benefited indirectly from the forest expansion. Pine martens declined greatly because of persecution in the previous century, but their numbers have recovered in many forest areas where there is no longer gamekeeping. Badgers and foxes have moved into the plantations wherever there is sufficient cover and food and suitable sites for setts or earths. Indeed farmers next to the forests at times feel they have become too good a home for rabbits and foxes which they view as a nuisance.

For a while red squirrels maintained a good hold in the big coniferous forests at Cannock and Thetford, despite losing ground to greys elsewhere in southern England. However, as more broadleaves spread or are planted in these forests they may yet give way to the grey. So should the spread of broadleaves, which do allow richer bird, plant and insect populations to develop in these plantations, be limited in the hope of encouraging red squirrels? In practice I think that little can be done for red squirrels in the lowlands of mainland Britain so that the wider conservation benefits of encouraging oak and birch among the pine should be pursued. In the north of more import may be the switch to greater areas of Sitka spruce and less pine in plantations of the future. The red squirrel has been thought to rely on mature pine crops for much of its food in these forests. Whether it can survive on Sitka spruce cones as readily as it does on Norway spruce on the Continent remains to be seen.

Undoubtedly the mammals that have gained most from the expansion of forestry have been deer, particularly red deer. Originally these were forest animals in Britain but they came to live mainly on open hills in Scotland simply because there were few forests left. Here they were encouraged so that they could be stalked for sport. Now they are moving back into forests and seem to do better there than on open moorland.

Many forests are deer-fenced when the trees are first planted, but it is difficult to maintain such fences and keep the deer out. New deer fences, which have to be high and impenetrable, are unpopular because they restrict access for humans too and detract from the local views. Rides and glades and clear-fell areas provide the main feeding areas but even in thicket stands there may be sufficient gaps to provide food for many animals. The explosion in deer numbers poses a threat to the regeneration of the forest itself. Deer also threaten other work that might be done to aid nature conservation. For example they make it much more difficult to establish native broadleaved trees to diversify upland forests, because, given the choice between young birch and young Sitka spruce, the deer browse the birch.

Attractive as deer may be, they need to be controlled, usually through shooting. Coping with deer is going to be a major problem for foresters in the 1990s and will include dealing not only with red, but also in places roe, fallow and sika deer.

Recently there has been much interest in the use of forests by bats. Since they are insectivorous, they need sufficient variety of vegetation, especially open or wet areas, to support good populations of flying insects. They are often found hunting along rides. Many would naturally have roosted in holes and under the loose bark of old trees but such places are rare in the young pine and spruce plantations. Like some birds, therefore, bats can be encouraged by putting up special bat boxes, but the first step must be to ensure that there are enough insects for them to feed on.

Insects and other groups

We know little about the insects and other groups of plants and animals in recent plantations so it is difficult to assess the gains and losses for nature conservation. The indications are that it is mainly the species already common that have spread. For the time being it may be sufficient to use the plants in the forest as a rough guide to the likely value of the area for insects, but in the longer term this must be matched by more surveys.

One group of species that has become more common as a result of forestry's expansion has been those that feed on the crop trees. A few of these have taken to the new plantations with a vengeance and have created major problems for foresters. The pine beauty moth lives chiefly on Scots pine where it does little damage, but has now spread to the great stands of lodgepole pine in the north of

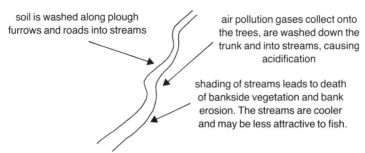

soil is washed along plough furrows and roads into streams

air pollution gases collect onto the trees, are washed down the trunk and into streams, causing acidification

shading of streams leads to death of bankside vegetation and bank erosion. The streams are cooler and may be less attractive to fish.

Ways in which forest plantations have adversely affected the wildlife of upland streams.

Scotland. Thousands of trees were killed before the outbreaks were controlled by spraying the forests at risk from the air with a pesticide. This is a potentially dangerous solution because other insects, birds and fish could be affected directly by the pesticide or, indirectly, by eating the poisoned caterpillars. As yet no serious side-effects of this programme on other wildlife have been reported.

More recently Sitka spruce in the Welsh Borders has come under attack from the spruce bark beetle, a species that is common on the Continent. There are hopes that these outbreaks can be controlled, not by insecticides, but by releasing another insect that attacks the bark beetle, a form of biological control.

It could still happen that, just as the spruce bark beetle arrived and remained undetected for several years, other pests may emerge as these new forests go through their second and third generations. The large, fairly even-aged forests mainly composed of one species that British foresters are creating are not dissimilar to some natural conifer forests in North America. In these, large-scale attack and killing of trees by insects (often associated with devastating fires, because the dead trees burn very easily) occur naturally, so perhaps this type of problem in British forests should not come as a surprise.

Effects on streams and watercourses

Many early plantations were around reservoirs in the uplands. One intention was to reduce public access to the catchment since this could be a threat to the purity of the water which received little treatment before it was used. Now most water has to be treated anyway and since forests may reduce considerably the yield of water from a catchment, there is less such planting.

More recently concern has arisen over the effects of coniferous forests on the quality of the water flowing in forest streams. Many streams and lakes in the uplands have been getting more acid; they no longer support fish; the abundance of insects and other invertebrate life in them has changed; and that characteristic bird of upland streams, the dipper, is unable to breed successfully on them. In some cases acidification started over a century ago and is a consequence of the industrial pollution that has eliminated Sphagnum moss on the tops of Pennine hills and most lichens from Epping Forest (Essex).

Air pollution may be the ultimate cause, but in some upland lakes there has been a marked increase in the rate of acidification over the last fifty years, coinciding with the major expansion of forestry in upland areas. Acidification is also worse in many forest streams compared to nearby ones flowing through moorland. Such studies are not conclusive evidence that the forests are causing higher acidification: in some instances the forests were planted on ground that was more acid to start with. However the trees do 'catch' more of the air-borne pollutants on their needles than the heather or grass that they replace and this then finds its way into the stream system. On some sites the ploughing and draining of peat may initiate other chemical reactions in the soil, which add to the acidifying process. Since forests can exacerbate stream and lake acidification on the poorest soils it seems prudent not to plant large areas of new forest where this is a risk. Just how extensive such high-risk areas are and where they occur is a matter for debate, but some research would lead to restrictions on planting in much of Wales and western Scotland.

Other effects of forests on streams are not disputed by foresters. Shading inhibits vegetation growth in the stream and lowers the water temperature; there are fewer invertebrates and hence probably fish. Plants on the stream bank are shaded out and the banks may become unstable; this leads to bank erosion and more sediment being washed downstream.

Sediment from bankside erosion and that washed into the streams following poor ploughing and work on forest roads has worried both ecologists and water authorities. Silt fills the space between the gravel in salmon and trout spawning beds and so fewer young fish are produced. Where the stream contributes to a water supply more expensive water treatment is needed. Such problems have led to the introduction of new guidelines to keep planting back from streamsides in the uplands. The whole range of streamside plant and animal communities should benefit from these recommendations provided that they are implemented.

Future rotations

The large, even-aged coniferous forests planted over the last fifty years should become more varied in future partly through deliberate management, partly by unplanned events, such as when large areas get blown down by wind. In Kielder Forest (Northumberland) in the second rotation there will be a range of stand sizes from 5-20 hectares in the valley bottoms, 25-50 hectares on the mid-slopes and 50-100 hectares on the upper slopes.

In forests on mineral soils there is a good chance that woodland plants and animals will become much more common where the trees can be thinned. On the upland peats however, where most recent planting has occurred, there is little indication that the life under the trees is any richer second time around. In these forests nature conservation efforts should be concentrated on making the most of open ground, both that created through felling and that found between the stands of trees. We may however find that the bird life of plantations is of more interest than previously acknowledged.

Is there another way?

During the last decade a new card entered the forestry pack in the form of European overproduction of some farm crops. Farmers are to be encouraged to stop growing food on some land and forestry is an alternative use. Whether foresters will get the chance to move down from the hills on any scale remains to be seen. Even if there is an expansion of lowland forestry in this way there is no guarantee that it will reduce the pressure to continue with the upland planting that has characterized the last fifty years.

Nevertheless in future a greater proportion of new plantations may be on a smaller scale and on different types of site from those created in the last fifty years. The effects of such small woods particularly on farms is considered later.

Room for improvement

Plantations of introduced conifers do not make much contribution to the conservation of our native woodland communities at present. With a few exceptions it seems unlikely that that position will change greatly in future. These forests are the source of most of our home-produced timber and their growth must remain fairly tightly controlled if managers are to meet production targets.

Nevertheless the pattern of large-scale felling and regeneration that is typical of the vast majority of these forests parallels the natural catastrophes that shape natural conifer woods in North America or northern Europe. Comparison between what happens in these natural forests and what has been learnt about managing plantations for wildlife in ancient woods can be used to improve these huge areas for wildlife. More could be made of open ground within the forests; trees in sheltered places could be left to grow on to their full lifespan; broadleaves could be encouraged more where there are suitable soils.

These large conifer forests are one of the main contributions of the twentieth century to the future landscape; our descendants may view them and their wildlife in a different light. By today's criteria, however, they are generally of limited nature conservation value and, if in the wrong place, the cause of considerable harm; poor substitutes for the legacy of semi-natural vegetation of which we are the temporary stewards.

7

Bluebells Amongst the Bricks, Woods Among the Wheat

Fiby Urskog is a primeval woodland in central Sweden, a rare survival in the south of a country where forestry is a major industry. What is more remarkable is that it is not in some remote mountain valley but about 16 km west of Uppsala. Britain can claim nothing quite like that, but from the top of a tower block in most cities you can see a surprising number of pockets of green trees in streets and gardens, old parks and fragments of ancient woodland, scrub and young woods developing on old railway lines or cemeteries. Most of us live in the middle of urban forests and their extent is set to increase dramatically under new ideas for planting in and around towns. Such new planting will merge with what is already under way on farms throughout the country.

Local people and planners increasingly recognize the opportunities offered by these relicts of the countryside within towns and by the new plantings. By the end of 1990, for example, the Forest of Cardiff project had put in 60,000 trees and involved 10,000 people in over 150 schemes. Unfortunately these new initiatives have not removed the threat to woods from new roads, quarries and housing developments. A challenge of the '90s will be whether such pressures can be controlled.

Woods in and around towns and cities

One of the first moves in modern conservation in Britain was the acquisition of Epping Forest in 1878 by the City of London. They wanted to protect it from destruction because it was an important place for Londoners who wanted a day out in the country. Since then the expansion of London has brought the town to the forest, the south-western part of which is now almost entirely surrounded by suburbs, but the forest still remains a place for enjoyment and relaxation. On the other side of the capital Burnham Beeches was acquired shortly after for similar reasons. The Ruislip woods are owned by Hillingdon Borough and Oxleas Wood in the south by Greenwich. To the north, Ken Wood on Hampstead Heath is only about four hectares in size but, despite the 1987 storm, still provides Londoners with an opportunity to see trees larger than are found in most nature reserves. In Willesden there are even the remnants of the hedges from around the fields on which the houses were built.

It is not only in the capital that woods survive: on the edge of Birmingham lies Sutton Park, a survival of a medieval landscape. Some of its coppices have been replanted, but there are still open heathy grazings and old pollards – a New Forest in miniature. Dunham Massey deer park just outside Manchester is an important site for beetles that live in dead wood. Thorpe Wood in

Peterborough, Kings Wood in Corby, Brasenose Wood in Oxford, Craig Pont Rhondda next to Tonypandy and Great Wood, Hadleigh, near Southend are among the more obvious urban survivals. How many other apparently undistinguished groves that might trace their history back to the wildwood are still lurking at street corners?

In the past such survivals were largely accidental – the town grew around and absorbed the wood or hedge. Now in new developments there are often conscious efforts to retain such features, as at Bar Hill (Cambridgeshire) or on a much grander scale in Milton Keynes. There the ancient woods within the new city limits have not only been kept but studied extensively. Management plans have been prepared, and seem to be successful, including fitness trails for humans and glades for wildlife.

A mixed blessing

Some ancient woods in or near towns have fared better than those in the heart of the country over the last fifty years. On the whole there has been less pressure to convert them to conifer plantations, because their value for recreation or as attractive places to look at is so obvious and far outweighs any commercial timber potential.

Urban woods do present a challenge however for the manager who is also concerned to keep them attractive for wild plants and animals. Just the pressures of people using the woods may literally wear away the plants and compact or erode the soil. The local residents may be so attached to their local wood that any management that involves cutting trees is greeted with horror. Coppicing work or the restoration of pollards as in Epping and Hainault Forests requires a very careful public relations exercise first, so that everyone knows what is going on, and why and how the wildlife is expected to benefit.

Public interest and involvement can then be turned to advantage. About half the newly planted trees in urban areas die within ten years because of lack of care. If local people are involved and regard the trees as theirs, then they may take steps to discourage vandalism, perhaps make sure the trees are watered in hot weather, to try to reduce the losses. In the same way, the more that people can be involved in community woodland management, the more likely it is that an urban wood will survive.

Other challenges arise because while rightly (or in some cases wrongly) urban woods are regarded as public open space, not everyone makes use of that space in socially acceptable ways. Some woods become the haunt of glue-sniffers so 'something' has to be done. Unfortunately 'something' may mean the complete removal of the understorey so that people can see from one side to the other. The shrubby cover needed by many nesting birds is destroyed; woodland herbs are suppressed by vigorously growing grasses. (Not that this or much else in woodland management is new. In the early Middle Ages woods were regarded as harbouring undesirables such as outlaws and wolves and so were cleared to a bowshot back from the roads.) Clearance of the understorey took place at Hangman's Wood, Essex, and for a while it was short mown grass, but it has now been left to grow a bit and there are at least the beginnings of new bramble thickets.

Urban woods are often the dumping ground for anything from old cars and supermarket trolleys to litter and garden rubbish. Bottles trap small mammals; sacks of litter smother the ground flora underneath and enrich the soil so that a swarm of nettles appears; oil seeps from old cars and contaminates local streams. Even if it does little long-term damage, litter may offend our eyes and feelings. It suggests a wood that nobody loves and that can be the first step towards its clearance.

Ironically, the rubbish left by woodmen of the nineteenth century counts as industrial archaeology and is prized! A rusting tractor left in a wood may in a hundred years' time cause as much excitement as the half-finished millstone that I found below the gritstone edge in Derbyshire. People study the medicinal herbs found in woods near to ruined monasteries, the distribution of nettles in relation to old buildings or rubbish heaps. Ecologists of the twenty-first century may write theses on the distribution of monbretias which frequently turn up in woods by roads, grown up from dumped garden rubbish, but it would be better if no rubbish were dumped in the first place.

The survival of ancient woods and those that have established naturally in recent years in towns is however always uncertain. Such undeveloped land often seems to be the most convenient place to put new roads, houses or factories. These pressures then spill over into the rest of the country through the demand for stone, sand and gravel.

Before the bulldozers

Very few of us are privileged enough to live in the middle of a wood and it is not surprising that developers should often come forward with schemes that use woods as the setting for new houses. So we lose yet another bit of woodland and its wildlife. Strong local opposition to this sort of development can succeed at public inquiries – as for example with the various proposals that there have been for parts of the Sydenham Hill Woods in south London which resulted in them being declared a local nature reserve by Southwark Council. The London Wildlife Trust and local people successfully fought to save the birch scrub at Gunnersbury Triangle, which was just a tiny pocket of recent woodland, just as the people of Birmingham had earlier saved Moseley Bog with its willow scrub.

It can be more difficult to deal with proposals that just take a small part of a relatively large, straggly wood. Along the shores of Loch Sunart in Lochaber some of the finest oakwoods in Britain, rich in rare mosses, lichens and liverworts, stretch down to the lochside road. Perhaps only a handful of trees need to be felled to make space for a house for a local worker, but this too matters. Even in the most rural parts of Britain large semi-natural woods are rare, and nibbling away at them makes them rarer still. Over the last fifty years such piecemeal attrition has accounted for an area many times larger than the largest semi-natural wood left in England.

It is not just the direct clearance of woodland that affects the wildlife. When a large wood is split into two by a road or a new quarry there are many indirect effects. The trees along the new edge are exposed to the wind, whereas before they were protected by their neighbours: they are more likely to blow over. Drainage lines through the wood may be cut; upslope the ground becomes wetter, because the water is held back by the road; roots die because there is less air in the soil and the trees become unstable; downslope pools and streams lose part of their source of water and are more likely to dry up. Dust and fumes increase in a band next to the road; salt and oil may be washed into the wood and some plants may die as a consequence. New sites for rubbish dumping are created by lay-bys.

Some birds are sensitive to traffic noise and may not breed as well in the new edge zone. An estimated 47,000 badgers a year are killed on roads as well as myriads of smaller creatures. Mammals such as mice and voles, and insects (even flying ones like moths) do not like to cross the wide open space which to them the road represents. We do not know in most cases what the long-term effects of this woodland fragmentation and the dividing up of populations will be, but the smaller the population of a species the less its chances for long-term survival.

Some but not all of these problems can be mitigated through good road design, for example by providing underpasses for badgers and by channelling run-off from the road so that it does not go straight into woodland streams. It would be preferable, however, to route the road elsewhere in the first place so that it does not destroy or fragment any woodland.

Given that we have to have roads, what price are we prepared to pay to safeguard our woodland heritage? More than we have in the past?

The route of the recent extension to the M40 was shifted to avoid it cutting through the Bernwood Forest, one of our richest butterfly sites. However the M25 cut through about half a dozen woods between Reigate and Orpington. The Knaresborough bypass bisects Birkham Wood; improvements to the A82 took out parts of the Loch Lomond oakwoods. The Channel Tunnel approaches obliterated a whole wood. There was a long planning inquiry into the route of a new road and river crossing in East London. Despite a final appeal to the European Commission on this site, the outcome is that a huge cutting will be made through part of Oxleas Woods. A battle is just starting over the route for the Arundel bypass, which would currently go through a nature reserve.

Roads and buildings need sand, gravel and stone. There has long been an association between woods and mineral working – the woods providing props for the mines or fuel for processing the material once it was dug. Small hollows, abandoned tunnels and the like are quite common in woods and on a small scale may add to their overall richness.

Today's workings tend to be on a much larger scale, often virtually removing a whole wood, perhaps leaving just a fringe of trees as a screen. Charndon Wood (Buckinghamshire) became just a large hole in the ground. What's left of Asham Wood (Somerset) has stood for thirty years on the brink of an extension to the adjacent quarries. Garth Wood (Glamorgan) is similarly poised. Parts of

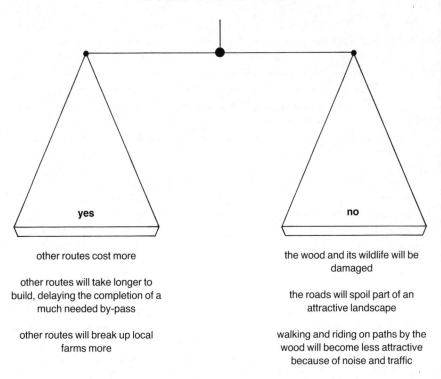

yes	no
other routes cost more	the wood and its wildlife will be damaged
other routes will take longer to build, delaying the completion of a much needed by-pass	the roads will spoil part of an attractive landscape
other routes will break up local farms more	walking and riding on paths by the wood will become less attractive because of noise and traffic

Birkham Wood balance sheet: Should the road go through the wood? There is seldom an easy answer.

the Halling Woods (Kent) have been earmarked to be dug for chalk. A rare landscape of small woods and fields is at risk in Carmarthen and with it a history of lime burning perhaps unique in Wales. What makes this last case so irksome is that the quarrying for limestone was proposed under an Interim Development Order granted before 1950, still valid in the very different social and economic conditions of the 1990s.

Ironically one of the richest woods in the country for flowers has perhaps been saved not once but twice by mining. Bedford Purlieus near Peterborough is close to the site of Roman potteries and was probably deliberately kept as woodland by them to provide the fuel for the kilns. Otherwise it might have been cleared for farming. Then some forty years ago the rights to the ironstone underneath it were acquired by a steel company. The Forestry Commission for a long time was unwilling to carry out major planting in it, because it was likely to be dug up before they could have harvested the trees. So the wood escaped the spruce blankets laid down in many of the Commission's other Rockingham Forest properties. Fortunately the ore proved of poor quality and later British Steel relinquished the rights.

Holes in the ground are a valuable asset these days to those who own them, if they can be filled with rubbish from nearby towns. Others fill up with water. Relatively few old quarries are likely to be allowed to scrub up and revert to woodland by natural succession. This is a pity, because the woodland so formed can be rich, albeit no substitute for any ancient woodland that may have been lost when the quarry was first created. One reason why such woods are so varied is that the new wood is developing on very poor soil, sometimes almost bare rock. Tree and shrub growth is irregular, different species invade at different places, and some patches remain open for a long time. This has implications for urban tree planting. On derelict ground there may be no need to dig holes and fill them with earth to get trees going: birch will seed happily into almost pure brick rubble and clinker.

New woods for wildlife

Milton Keynes is noted not just for the retention of its existing ancient woods, but for the extent of new planting that has taken place along roads and between the different settlement centres. Such new planting, including that along motorway verges, is a feature of many other new developments. Some is done with the normal commercial timber species. There are places where that is wholly appropriate, although planting tall, fast-growing species such as spruce or Douglas fir along roads or close to houses may create problems when these need to be thinned or felled. Smaller or slower growing trees and shrubs may fit into the landscape better and be better for wildlife. Species that grow naturally in a particular region and on a particular soil are preferable – ash, field maple and hawthorn for heavy clay soils in the south, birch and rowan for acid sands, alder and sallows for wet areas.

'Natural' type planting schemes that try to match the trees and shrubs to the local area have been tried at Milton Keynes, Warrington and Peterborough new towns and are likely to become more common. Trees and shrubs are only the 'skeleton' of a wood; some birds and insects move in quickly, but it may take a long while for flowers such as bluebells and primroses to arrive if left to themselves. The process might be speeded up by planting woodland herbs along with or shortly after the trees. Provided they are common species that might be expected to grow anyway on that soil type there is little reason not to try this on a small scale. Work on this is still in its infancy; we do not know enough about the best soil conditions for some of these plants, whether to introduce them at the start or wait till the trees have grown a bit first. It may be that in the long-run the survival rate is so low that it is not worth the costs of the process. Trials and experiments are needed to find out.

When there is no chance of stopping the destruction of a wood, another idea is that some of the species in it should be transferred to a new site. Experiments with this have been tried, by shifting soil and even coppice stools; taking seed from the ground flora or the plants themselves and growing them on. Individually all these things can be done; the difficulty comes when you try to put the elements of a wood back on to a similar unwooded site elsewhere. Sadly, it is not so easy to re-assemble a wood as though it were a jig-saw. Any resemblance between the original and the new wood can be no more than literally superficial. Soil profiles built up over hundreds of years cannot be shifted undisturbed, even if the earth itself is moved. Some species of insects, fungi or mosses are bound to be lost in the process even if all the higher plants can be transferred. No matter how good a copy you make of the Mona Lisa it remains a copy, of less value than the real thing, and at present our skill at copying old woods is like that of a five-year-old with her first set of paints. What may be a more realistic aim is to liven up new woods by trying to build in more variety at the outset.

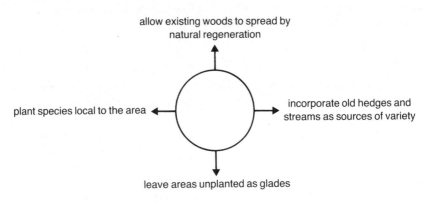

Livening up new woods.

Community forests and the New National Forest

The forest area of Britain may have doubled this century but very little of that expansion has occurred near to the main centres of population. This is understandable since in the lowlands, where most people live, farming has generally been more profitable than forestry; but it is unfortunate since forests can perform a dual function – grow trees and also provide an environment where people can relax and enjoy themselves. Forests also help to heal the scars on the landscape left by past industries; the pit heaps of South Wales valleys are being clad now by trees.

One aim of the 1985 policy for broadleaved woodland was to encourage broadleaved planting around towns and cities. The Countryside Commission for England and Wales and the Forestry Commission followed this up with proposals for new community forests on the edges of our great urban sprawls. Twelve areas are being considered initially, from Swansea to Cleveland, of which three, in south Tyne and Wear, east London and south Staffordshire, are already being developed. Each may eventually spread to some fifteen square miles. Even grander schemes exist to produce a New National Forest near Leicester. This is to be on the scale of the New Forest in Hampshire, and is being created in the region of the old royal forest of Charnwood. Areas of old industrial dereliction are to be transformed into a mixture of woods and open areas. In Scotland a similar idea is under way to create a forest in the central belt between Glasgow and Edinburgh, to soften its rather bleak landscapes. New jobs may be created in the process.

All these initiatives will involve a mixture of private and public ownership. It is hoped that there will be a high proportion of broadleaved planting as well as areas left to regenerate naturally. Some commercial stands of conifers or broadleaved-coniferous mixtures will help to drive the project along by producing a faster return from the timber crop. As far as nature conservation is concerned this should not be so much of a drawback as recent upland afforestation; a stand of Douglas fir may not be as good for wildlife as one of oak but it is likely to be of more interest than the arable fields on which much of this planting will take place. Even in the most uniform of forests there is usually more variety of plants and animals, less use of fertilizers and herbicides than in a barley field.

A key point about the design of these new forests should be that they complement and enhance existing areas which are good for wildlife, not replace or impoverish them. Species-rich grassland, wetland and heath should form the core of the new open areas and be protected from planting. Existing broadleaved woodland and hedges should be expanded using natural regeneration or by planting of appropriate native species to improve the links between sites. Fast-growing conifer crops established on land currently of little wildlife interest at present should help to stimulate local timber markets which in turn can provide an outlet for the produce from existing broadleaved woods.

New farmland plantings

As the new forest initiatives spread out from the city centres so they join up with other schemes to plant more trees on farmland to reduce the agricultural surpluses. The latter are not about landscape change on the grand scale, but through them many new woods, often small, are steadily appearing on farms. Corners fenced off or strips along a headland studded with tree shelters are often the tell-tale signs.

The government has produced a series of schemes to encourage the planting of woods on farms. The area planted so far under these schemes has been less than planned and, as with the larger new forests, there is always the risk that they may be planted in the wrong place. We are unlikely to see major nature conservation benefits coming from them for a long while yet but it may help to restore some of the links between surviving woods, hedges and old meadows.

In the past, getting farmers interested in trees and woods was often seen as one of the hurdles to improving the management of ancient and semi-natural woods. If there was ever a tradition of part-time farmers and part-time foresters in Britain similar to that in parts of Scandinavia, it has been lost. Wood is not so important as a rural fuel and it is rare to see the stacks of logs all up the side of the house under the eaves that you see in France. Now, for a variety of reasons – conservation, shelter, game and timber – farmers are much more aware of the trees and woods on their land. One area where it is particularly important to engage farmers' interest is where the woods are used for grazing for much of the year. The consequences and possible solutions to the over-grazing problem are explored in the next chapter.

8

Surviving by the Skin of the Teeth

Each year heather moors are burnt to encourage the supply of young shoots for grouse to eat. There are then more birds to be shot. In a similar way the plains Indians in North America altered the balance between prairie and forest by burning the prairie. This slowed or stopped the spread of trees so there was more grass for the buffalo which they hunted.

Perhaps our Mesolithic ancestors tried to do the same to increase the area of open grazing for their quarry, the deer and the wild ox. Unfortunately for them, most lowland broadleaved woods do not burn very well. Only on some dry acidic soils, where the canopy had been partially opened up already, perhaps by a windstorm, might there be enough of an accumulation of bracken, tall grasses and heather for ground fires to occur as they do on heaths or in the native pinewoods still remaining today. Burning to improve the grazing may thus have been important only in upland Britain.

Gaps in the forest, however, whether created deliberately or not, would tend to attract grazing animals, because there is more food available in them. Wild ox probably hung around glades and clearings most of the time as do the bison in Polish forests or the cattle in the New Forest. Deer move into glades to feed, but then go to denser areas of forest to lie up.

Teeth versus seedlings

Seedlings and saplings in such glades may be cropped with the grass during the summer and in winter may be the only food showing above the snow. They are not necessarily killed if they are eaten; many produce fresh shoots the next year, sometimes several all growing up from one place, resulting in a bushy shape. Some such seedlings, although less than 30 cm high, may be five or ten years old. However if they are eventually to become young trees the amount they grow each year must be more than the amount by which they are bitten back. Whether or not regeneration in forest gaps is successful depends on the balance between the numbers of animals grazing there and the vigour of the trees. If there are relatively few animals, and plenty of alternative areas where they can feed, then the clearing may close over rapidly. If many animals concentrate on just a few glades then regeneration there is impossible. Trees on the edge of the glade eventually die and the glade gets bigger.

In this shifting balance between the animals and regeneration it may not be what happens in the average year that is important. Two or three years' vigorous growth can be wiped out by just one winter of very heavy grazing; a few years' respite is all that is needed for the trees to grow tall enough for their terminal bud to be out of reach, even if heavy grazing is resumed thereafter.

The introduction of domestic animals

As farming in Britain developed and farms spread, so the wild animals that grazed in the forest were hunted out or their numbers greatly reduced; on the other hand, the numbers of domestic animals – horses, sheep and cattle – that needed to be fed increased. Woodland became restricted to small patches; most of the country in effect became one vast clearing. Uncontrolled grazing in what little woodland remained could not be allowed if the woods were to regenerate; the value of the firewood and timber was such that some way of protecting young tree growth had to be found, despite hungry beasts.

In coppice woods the regrowth must be protected in the first few years after a cut. Many coppices have old wood banks running round and through them which once had fences or hedges on top. Animals could be kept out of one part of the wood, but allowed free range elsewhere. Partitioning of the wood meant that there did not have to be a complete separation of farming and wood production. Open glades could be grazed or mown for hay; grazing animals could also be let into the parts of the wood where the coppice shoots had grown big enough not to be damaged by the animals. Cattle, by eating brambles and other tall plants, may even have made it easier for the woodmen when they next came to cut the coppice. Where woods were not divided, grazing might still have been possible since the animals could be controlled by shepherds and cowherds (or small children) in a way that is not possible today. Not that grazing always was precisely controlled, as frequent court cases from early medieval times onward testify.

The consequences of not controlling grazing or browsing cattle or deer, when they were abundant, would have been as serious then as now. Most stools throw up another set of shoots if the first are eaten back, but some may not and gaps develop in the coppice. The shoots that do appear have to compete with much denser growth of grass or bramble than occurs in the first year after cutting. This dense vegetation provides more food for the grazing animals, and is more attractive to them. It is more difficult to keep out cattle or deer once they have got used to feeding in an area than if they have never been allowed in.

Common grazing and pollards

There were in medieval times, and still are, woods on common land where fencing and controlled grazing were not possible. People had and have rights to turn out a number of animals into these woods and either it is not possible to get agreement to restrict them to particular areas or there are laws which mean that such fencing cannot take place. In the heyday of the Royal Hunting Forests there was also the need to let the monarch's deer roam unhindered.

Getting a sustained supply of wood from such areas was still desirable, but coppicing was out of the question. Instead the trees were cut at 2-3 m above the ground. If this is done while the tree is relatively young (when the trunk is less than 30 cm across) new poles grow out from just below the cut surface and the regrowth is out of reach of cattle and deer. When they reach a suitable size the poles can be cut, a new set grows from the trunk and the process may be repeated indefinitely rather as with coppicing. Most broadleaved trees will respond to this treatment, which is known as pollarding. It is still commonly used on streamside willows and trees in towns, in the latter case simply to keep the branches and the crown of the tree small.

The lopped branches provided poles and firewood as did those from coppice, but there may also have been some much more frequent cutting of the branches for fodder. Leaves and young twigs of birch were used in Norway for winter cattle feed until recently and those of elm and ash are even more nutritious. Holly, despite its prickles, might be lopped for deer, and was used as winter feed for sheep in, among other places, the Lake District.

The pollard solution was adopted in a wide range of circumstances and, even if they have not been cut for many years, pollards are readily recognizable. They have squat low trunks, often partially rotten, and several massive branches all coming out from the one point. They can be found in hedgerows and on the edges of coppice woods, on old commons such as Ebernoe in Sussex, in deer parks such as Dynefor in Dyfed or Dalkeith in Lothian and in the old Royal Hunting Forests (where these retain any trees), like the New Forest (Hants) and Epping (Essex).

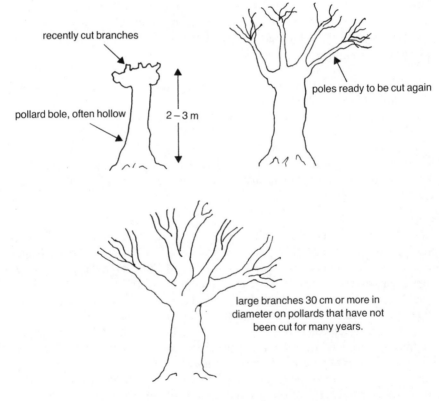

Pollard trees.

Areas with old pollards may not be grazed now. Natural regeneration t. runs riot, often of dense holly, and the pollards may be hidden among muc young growth.

Effects on the wood

A wood may look quite dense, but bend down to the height a deer can reach conveniently (about four foot for a fallow) or ask a small child what it looks like from her level. Often it is much more open and there is a clear browse line below which all the leaves and thin twigs or branches have been eaten. Saplings and young trees may be killed in this way; even larger trees may die if their bark is stripped or rubbed off all the way round the tree.

Deer, cattle and sheep prefer to eat some plant species more than others, so palatable species such as lime or hazel are particularly vulnerable to grazing. Where grazing is high the constituents of a wood will be changed and more distasteful trees will tend to increase. In Lady Park Wood (Gwent) deer seem to have preferred beech to birch when they were feeding among the dense young trees that were growing up in the early '50s so that the latter came to be prominent in the canopy today. However even Scots pine and Sitka spruce with its sharp needles will be taken if the deer are hungry enough.

For a long while the canopy in a wood that is over-grazed may remain unbroken; from a distance the wood appears healthy. However, as trees die, are felled or fail to regrow after pollarding, there are no saplings waiting to shoot up to fill the gaps. The wood eventually becomes like a park and, as individual trees are lost, so a bit more of the wood ceases to exist.

Places like the New Forest survive, despite being grazed heavily for centuries, because every now and then there is a burst of successful regeneration. Seedlings and saplings do not have to be produced each year to ensure the replacement of the existing cover. As long as, over the life-time of each oak or beech or pine, on average one seedling is produced that grows through to become a mature tree, then the continuity of the wood is ensured. Oak and beech do not produce a lot of seed each year, but in some years there are thousands on one tree. Combine such a good year with a period when the grazing density is low and there is the chance for regeneration, even though there may have been none for decades previously.

In the New Forest the distinct differences in the sizes of the oaks suggest there was a major burst of regeneration between 1650 and 1750 when stock were controlled; it happened again from 1858-1915 following removal of deer from the Forest. Thus each of the old generations of trees originated during a period when there seem to have been fewer animals in the Forest. There has been a further burst of regeneration from about 1938, although it is not so clear why.

Effects of pollarding on trees

The pollarding of trees in parks, forests and commons has had the effect of prolonging the life of the trunk. In part this is because the trunk of a pollard grows more slowly than that of an ordinary tree. Every time the pollard is cut it has to produce a new set of leaves and branches and for a while will be able to absorb less energy and manufacture less sugars for growth than the full tree. Slow-growing trees, whether or not they are pollards, tend to live longer than fast-growing ones.

Pollards are also likely to be rotten inside. Water accumulates in the top of the trunk in hollows left where the branches have been cut and there are many open surfaces that allow fungi in to break down the heartwood. Losing your heart may not seem like a recipe for long life, but for a tree the wood at the centre may have little function – the transport of nutrients and water from the roots to the leaves and of sugars in the opposite direction is done by the outer sapwood and inner bark. Getting rid of the dead wood (literally) leaves the tree with an outer cylinder which is lighter and more flexible than a solid trunk. It may even be better able to stand up to major storms.

Stag-headed trees – where the tops of major branches die, but the foliage lower down remains healthy – also live on for centuries. Thus to describe a hollow tree or one with a few dead limbs as being on its way out may be a narrow anthropocentric view. Rather perhaps the tree is being economical, discarding material that is no longer of much use to it.

The rottenness at the centre of a pollard is also of immense importance for nature conservation. The flies, beetles, pseudoscorpions, fungi and other creatures that relied on dead and dying wood in the original forests now most commonly occur in such trees. Those old oaks and beeches of the New Forest, Sherwood or Windsor Great Park may look strange to us, but some of our rarest insects home in on them. Indeed some species are only found in or around just a handful of trees. If those trees are lost, through storm or the desire to tidy up dead wood, then we may lose one more relict of the wildwood. The violet click beetle at Windsor Forest (one of our rarest species) may not be of much use to anyone, but to let it become extinct in Britain would be a sign of poor stewardship of our natural heritage.

Another group of species that are often abundant on old pollards are the lichens. In the east they have suffered much from air pollution. Places like Epping Forest, once renowned, are now deserts for them. Elsewhere, particularly in the north-west, they thrive and may be found on even quite young trees, some as grey or black dots on the bark, others as crusts and the most spectacular as fronds and beard-like growths. Many lichens must also not become too shaded, hence they like the open conditions of parkland and the relatively light shade cast by pollard canopies.

Where were these lichens when most of Britain was a forest? They may have been as rare then as now, but for different reasons, living only on trees on the edge of permanent clearings. Perhaps their occurrence is a sign that much of the wildwood was more open than we imagine. Perhaps they grew much higher up the trees when the air was cleaner and rain less acid. They may have grown on the main branches and upper trunks of forest giants that stood out from patches of younger growth, when the surrounding trees had been blown down by storms or had collapsed through disease or root rot. We do not know.

Rottenness is all very fine for conservation; but, by law, an owner may be liable for damage or injury caused by falling branches or trunks. Hence owners may be obliged to tackle trees showing signs of major decay or structural weakness, particularly if they are close to paths or roads. Wherever possible, however, old trees should receive the respect due to their age. Only trim back what is necessary.

Below the canopy

Just as some trees and shrubs are more likely than others to be eaten by deer, cattle and sheep so there are differences among the ground flora. Brambles, tall broad-bladed grasses, herbs and bilberry are among the first species to be eaten. Ivy and honeysuckle retreat to rocks or cliffs where they are out of reach. A close-cropped turf, dominated by grasses with narrow leaves and unpalatable species such as bracken, may be left. In the west of Britain there is often also a luxuriant carpet of mosses, which grow better once the shade from the taller herbs and grasses has been removed, but are not themselves particularly nutritious. Along paths and where animals come together the ground becomes trampled and bare or invaded by weeds such as docks and chickweed.

Eating away the tall herbs that provide ground cover may reduce the density of small mammals, which in turn means less food for predators such as buzzards. Fewer shrubs, young trees and saplings means fewer nest sites for small birds. Over hundreds of years the soil itself may become poorer as nutrients are taken up by the plants, absorbed by the cattle and sheep and then lost from the site when the beasts drop their dung or are slaughtered elsewhere.

Dung left in the wood on the other hand provides another specialized habitat that some beetles and other invertebrates can exploit.

Maintaining wood-pasture

Traditional wood-pasture management, the mixture of grazing animals and pollarded trees, like coppicing, has gone into decline – and for similar economic reasons; but its value for nature conservation has not perhaps been widely appreciated. When they were actively managed the branches would have been small enough to be lopped with an axe. Most of the pollards we see now have not been cut for many years. They look picturesque, but there is a risk that the whole tree will split apart because the branches have become too big or unbalanced for the trunk. A chain saw is needed to cut them and a difficult and dangerous job it is too. Even then it is not certain that these old trees will regrow, so is it worth the effort?

Old hornbeams have been repollarded successfully by the National Trust at Hatfield, and elsewhere managers are learning the best ways to deal with oak

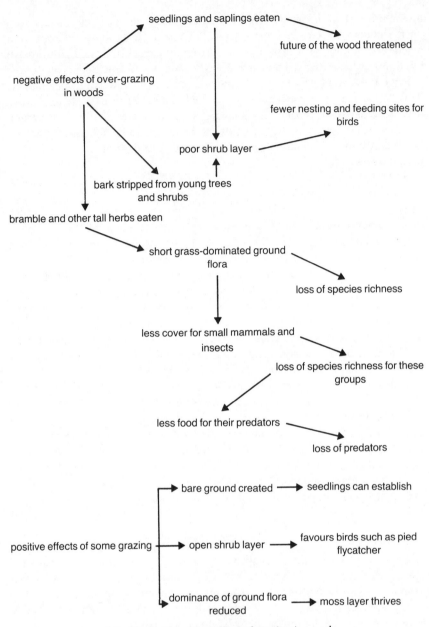

Negative and positive effects of grazing in woods.

and beech. The trick with beech may be to cut in summer and not to cut all the branches off at one time. Instead, one is left on if it can be done without unbalancing the tree, and this improves the chances that new shoots will develop from the main trunk. Although the poles cut from pollards would formerly have been taken away to be used, the big cut branches from a major repollarding should be left close to the trunk, preferably in long grass or bracken in partial shade. These branches are often part rotten and themselves have become home to species previously restricted to the trunk.

We should also start a new generation of pollards where there are presently only very old ones. Selected trees of the same range of species should be cut when their trunks are about 15-30 cm across. These may look ugly at first, but eventually they will form the next generation of incredible hulks. It will probably take at least a hundred years before they are in the right state to be invaded by the more fastidious of our deadwood insects and fungi.

The larvae of these beetles live in dead wood but the adults often feed on nectar. Encouraging hawthorns and other native flowering shrubs, patches of bramble and other flowers of old parkland is thus also desirable. Where there is no prospect of natural regeneration (because of grazing), planting mixed groups of trees and shrubs should be encouraged.

Getting some new trees, shrubs and more of a ground flora usually requires less grazing, but there is a danger in too much young growth on some of these sites as well as too little. Dense regeneration around old pollards shades out lichens on the lower trunks and eventually the young trees overtop and kill the pollards themselves. Retaining a combination of some grazing and some young trees is likely to be the best option – keeping fairly close in fact to how these sites were formerly treated.

Woods as sheep shelters

Throughout western Britain there are woods mainly of oak and birch, often formerly coppiced, that are now heavily overgrazed and lack signs of regeneration.

Keeping animals out of coppices when the growth was young was probably always a problem. However, as the oak coppices of the west and upland birch woods lost timber value in the last century, there was no longer much incentive even to try. The woods still have a use as sheltered grazing, but in most cases no steps are taken to ensure that the wood will still be there to provide that shelter in the future. Matters have been made worse by the increase in the numbers of sheep and deer on the hills over the last 50 years.

Most of these woods were formerly coppiced and have been cut at least once in the last 100 years. Unlike in the wood pasture found in the old royal forests and commons there are not usually many big trees and old pollards in these upland grazed woods. They thus lack a good dead wood fauna, although they are often rich in lichens because they are in some of the cleanest air zones. More importantly the high rainfall found in the west makes them particularly good for mosses and liverworts.

Some mosses and liverworts are so sensitive to drying out that their presence may pinpoint areas which have never been completely cleared, such as ravines. Others rely on the shelter of rock overhangs to get them through the time between a wood being cut and the subsequent re-formation of the canopy. Upland woods include some of the most important sites for these plants not only in Britain, but in the world.

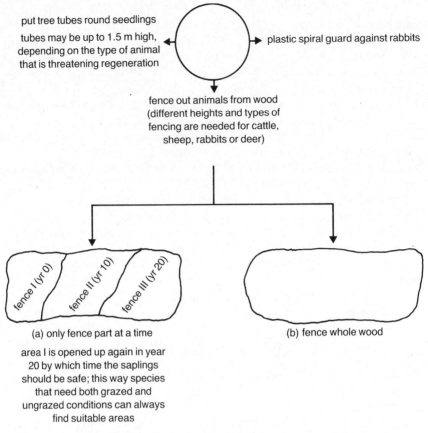

put tree tubes round seedlings

tubes may be up to 1.5 m high, depending on the type of animal that is threatening regeneration

plastic spiral guard against rabbits

fence out animals from wood (different heights and types of fencing are needed for cattle, sheep, rabbits or deer)

fence I (yr 0)   fence II (yr 10)   fence III (yr 20)

(a) only fence part at a time

(b) fence whole wood

area I is opened up again in year 20 by which time the saplings should be safe; this way species that need both grazed and ungrazed conditions can always find suitable areas

Protecting woods and trees.

Grazing brings mosses and liverworts into prominence because the tall grasses and herbs are suppressed, whereas sheep do not like eating mosses. The large species that form the luxuriant carpets and hummocks typical of woods in North Wales, Argyll or the Lake District are not necessarily the rarities. They are, however, a distinctive feature that should be conserved.

Most of these woods lack a shrub layer. When the woods were managed, often for tanbark and charcoal, shrubby species such as hazel would be cut at the same time as the oak. In some cases they were cut out because they were less valuable than the oak. Since the woods have been neglected the sheep or deer have prevented any understorey of shrubs or young trees getting re-established. This open space below the canopy has proved particularly attractive to wood warblers, redstarts and pied flycatchers, which may not be so abundant if the wood becomes denser.

There is a need to regenerate the woods, but also a case for keeping some grazing in the long run, for those species that benefit from grazed conditions. The shelter that the woods provide may be important to the hill farmers as well.

To achieve a mix of grazing levels the first thing to do is to
afresh the walls or fences that formerly kept the animals are
wood under control.

The fence and defence of grazed woods

Once you put a fence around a previously grazed wood and make sure
no large grazing animals left inside the changes can be dramatic. 'Seedlings', in
reality often several years old, previously barely showed above the grass because
they were bitten back each year. Now they grow 20 or 30 centimetres in a
season. Patches of bare ground sprout new birch seedlings. Oaks push up
through the mat of moss, litter and grass, but not everywhere. Other factors
may prevent regeneration.

Many of the trees of upland woods, including oak, birch and pine, need a lot
of light before their seedlings can grow to young trees. Thus they are only likely
to thrive in large gaps or where an area on the edge of a wood has been fenced.
Oak seedlings under oak trees may be stripped of their leaves by caterpillars
dropping from the canopy or develop mildew in the shade. Rowan and holly are
more capable of growing under shade and in the RSPB's Nagshead reserve in
the Forest of Dean there is a clear demonstration of this. Part of the wood was
fenced by the Forestry Commission forty years ago, part left open to the
traditional sheep grazing. The fenced area is now almost impenetrable.

Sometimes the best place to put up a fence is not within the wood but just
beyond its edge. There is plenty of light for the seedlings from the adjacent
wood and it helps to increase the area of land under trees. Frequently on
moorland there are already seedlings among the heather just waiting their
chance.

A change in the ground flora in fenced areas can also be apparent after only
one season. The plants grow taller; bramble, honeysuckle and ivy start to spread
down from refuges on rocks and out over the woodland floor making dense
tangles. Bilberry grows tall and lush. In the Morrone Birkwood an attractive
consequence of fencing out deer was the flowering of globe flowers. The dense
vegetation that develops once grazing stops may reduce the further
establishment of tree seedlings and compete with those already there. There is
also more cover for voles which eat seedlings. At this stage light grazing helps
the trees by taking away overshading leaves of bramble, grass or bilberry and
creating through trampling the occasional patch of bare ground in which new
seedlings can establish.

The species that thrive under heavily grazed conditions may lose out in the
ungrazed areas. Mosses are shaded out by dense herb layers, wood warblers can
no longer find bare woodland floor in which to nest, and in a dense shrub layer,
pied flycatchers may not be able to compete with bluetits.

All these species can be accommodated, since it is possible to get the
regeneration to secure the long-term future of these woods without necessarily
stopping all grazing all of the time. Parts of the wood can be fenced and then
opened to grazing again after 10-15 years. The pressure on the seedlings and

ings can be reduced by grazing only in winter or only in summer, or the number of animals in the wood could be reduced. Just as under the coppice cycle a mixture of open, regenerating and mature stands could be sustained in one wood, so in upland woods a different sort of cycle of fencing and regeneration is needed that will maintain their value to the upland farmer.

Deer on the loose

It is ironic that while in many wood pastures there are not enough stock to maintain the open ground, in many coppices the numbers of deer are now such that the coppice regrowth and seedling trees are being eaten. In Hayley Wood, Cambridgeshire, they have a penchant for the oxlip flowers. Only within the deer-fenced block do these still provide the dramatic displays for which the wood was well known.

There may be more deer now in lowland Britain than ever before, partly because they are not hunted as much, but also because there are many more fields of winter wheat around the woods which provide food for the deer in the lean months of the year. Roe deer, once virtually eliminated from the south, are spreading, as are fallow. These last were brought to Britain, probably by the Romans, as parkland animals, but have run wild. Another deer that has established itself in southern woods is the muntjac. Browse lines and deer paths are appearing in many woods for the first time this century. In parts of the country rabbits are also increasing after the decimation of their numbers caused by myxomatosis.

Different woods require different solutions to the grazing problem – electric fences, dead hedges where thorn and other thin branches are woven into a fence, piles of branches laid over the coppice stool – all may be encountered as well as conventional types of fencing. Seedlings can be protected using spiral guards against rabbits and tree shelters against small deer. Ultimately something is going to have to be done about the numbers of deer in the countryside if the rest of our woodland wildlife is not to suffer. Control – i.e. killing – seems to me inevitable. The longer it is delayed the heavier it will have to be unless we are to wait for starvation or disease to take a hand.

Twentieth-century wood-pasture?

There are few completely new ideas; most are rediscoveries of old ones which are then given new names. Coppice is being revived in a modern form as willow or poplar stands cut every two or three years, by machines like combine harvesters to be converted into chips for firewood. Deer are starting to be farmed, in some cases in medieval deer parks. Trials are also under way to see if there is scope for new forms of wood-pasture: growing sycamore or Sitka spruce at wide spacings with rye grass in between. The value for wildlife of very short rotation coppice or of such agro-forestry is likely to be low, however, and they should not be confused with their traditional counterparts.

9

Fun and Game in the Woods

The first people to hunt in the forests of Britain were concerned with getting their food as quickly and as easily as possible. However it would be surprising if they did not also feel some sense of awe for the land, the trees and animals as they went about their business. As the forests shrank so did our fears that we might become hopelessly lost, be devoured by wild beasts or set upon by outlaws, although such fears have not been totally dispelled and persist in children's literature and legend. Woods became places for enjoyment as well as places to work.

William I was said to love the high hart as a father, but the prime role of the Royal Hunting Forests was more mundane. They were sources of fresh meat, revenue and power. Still, hunting deer and boar were considered pleasures and the forests provided the quarry for the lords who held the rights. The medieval forests were not necessarily tree-covered, any more than a Scottish deer forest is today. Even villages and arable crops could fall within the bounds of the forest law. They were simply tracts of land wherein the king held particular rights pertaining to the deer, and to maintaining the conditions that the deer needed.

Culling deer from forests and deer parks gradually ceased to be an important source of meat even for the king. Deer are still hunted and shot and some may be eaten, but the emphasis has now changed. Hunting in woods is regarded primarily as a sporting activity and in the lowlands far more effort is put into the shooting of game birds, particularly pheasants, rather than deer.

Our taste in landscape has also changed. An open well tilled view (with the promise of much safe food) would have been very attractive to our distant ancestors. In turn, there have been fashions for imposing order and 'civilization' on the landscape, and then favouring 'wilderness' – which is the current favourite. There is however no such thing as totally natural woodland in Britain and striving for naturalness can require just as much effort by the forester, albeit differently directed, as does the creation of a well ordered garden.

Changes made to make the wood look right, or to improve it for fun and game affect the wild plants and animals that the wood contains, sometimes for the better, sometimes for the worse. There may be less frequent conflicts with nature conservation than if timber production is the prime aim, but conflict still occurs. Past persecution of large predators – both birds such as hawks and mammals such as the pine marten – has given gamekeepers a bad name. Other disadvantages of recreation in woods are discussed below.

A good sport?

In the latter Middle Ages a park with deer was something of a status symbol, and the vogue for game preserving on a grand scale that developed in the nineteenth century was just that – a vogue. It arose at a time when the former uses of many lowland coppice woods were in decline. Changes in farming practice and increased timber imports meant less need for hurdles or local grown oak for houses. Enclosures and the reallocation or extinction of common rights in woodland meant that it was easier for land owners to gain exclusive use of their woods, and these became private places, wherein pheasants could be reared or foxes encouraged.

Shooting is still very popular and many woods, particularly small woods on farms, have been retained through periods of agricultural intensification only because of their sporting value. Our countryside is the richer as a result.

Game management may have been the reason that the woods survived in the past, but there may be other ways of carrying them through to the twenty-first century. Both in Britain and abroad there is debate as to whether it is right to use hunting for sport as a means of paying for nature conservation. If the quarry species is threatened with extinction or if the hunting itself might disturb or kill a threatened species, there is no disputing that hunting should stop. Where, however, the quarry is a common or introduced species, reared specially for the purpose, as with pheasants, the rights and wrongs of hunting remain debatable. For the moment it remains legal and often forms a profitable use of woods.

Leaving morality aside, what are the effects of game management on the wildlife in the woods where it is practised?

Pheasants spend much of their time at the edges of woods. A scatter of small woods on a shoot is often better than one large one. Therefore many estates have planted small woods, rather as spinneys and coverts were created or encouraged by the fox-hunting squires of the nineteenth century. The value for wildlife of each individual little wood may be low, but they often include a higher proportion of native broadleaved trees than purely commercial plantations and collectively they help restore some of the losses of hedgerows and small copses over the last fifty years. Edges may be created inside the wood in the form of wide rides, which provide sheltered sunny places rich in flowers that are good for butterflies and other insects of the open woodland such as hoverflies.

The low shrubby cover that pheasants like within a wood may be increased by coppicing patches, with the consequence that small birds, many insects and flowers also flourish. Other small gaps may be created at points where the shooters stand and these can similarly increase the local species richness. The hedges that surround a wood may be maintained to give the pheasants more shelter and prevent the wood becoming too draughty. Such hedges also protect the woodland flora from effects of any drifting crop spray from the adjacent fields.

Less welcome from the nature conservation point of view is the introduction to semi-natural woods of conifers and shrubs such as rhododendron or snowberry to provide cover for the birds. These last two spread to form impenetrable thickets that hinder the beaters when they go through the wood, so are now less likely to be used. Rather than troubling to maintain a hedge round the wood farmers may put big straw bales round instead which can cover

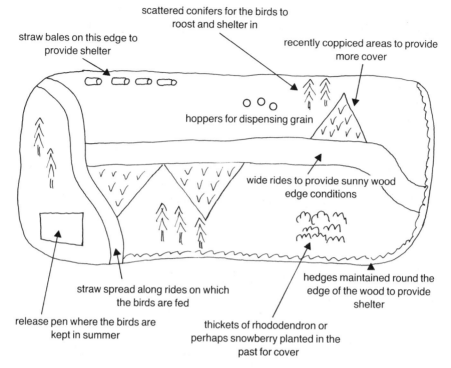

scattered conifers for the birds to
roost and shelter in

straw bales on this edge to
provide shelter

recently coppiced areas to provide
more cover

hoppers for dispensing grain

wide rides to provide sunny wood
edge conditions

hedges maintained round the
edge of the wood to provide
shelter

straw spread along rides on which
the birds are fed

release pen where the birds are
kept in summer

thickets of rhododendron or
perhaps snowberry planted in the
past for cover

Aspects of a shooting wood (not all present in any one site).

woodbanks and smother their often-rich plant life.

Although wild pheasants are generally reckoned to give the better sport, there may not be enough of them to justify the estate's investment in the shoot. Hence birds are reared and then released in the wood before the start of the shooting season. There may then be problems with the release pens and feeding rides. The release pens are where the birds are held when they are first brought to the wood. If too many birds are put into a pen at a time, not only are the birds more likely to get diseases, but the ground is stripped of most of its vegetation, as in a chicken coop. Weeds such as chickweed and docks invade the bare ground, which is enriched by the bird droppings and some woodland flowers such as ground ivy and yellow archangel disappear.

After the pheasants have been released from the pens the gamekeeper tries to encourage them to stay in particular woods and not to wander off on to the neighbouring estate. Grain is put out for them in hoppers or scattered among straw along rides. Such carpets of straw smother many of the plants on the ride particularly the smaller woodland herbs, such as wood-avens and violets. Some feeding along rides may be unavoidable if the wood is to be used for a shoot. One solution is then to feed but without putting down straw so that the effects on the ground flora are much less. The choice of which ride to use must be made very carefully, because the results may be as irreversible as when a forester decides to turn a ride into a hard core road to extract the coppice.

In the past keepers killed so many birds of prey and mammals such as pine martens and polecats that they became endangered. The list of species that may now be killed legally is much smaller and keepers are more enlightened, but stoats, weasels and hedgehogs may still be treated as 'vermin'. From a conservation point of view, native animals should not be killed to maintain artificially high levels of an introduced bird. The traditional habit of leaving the corpses to dangle on a gibbet can only reinforce prejudices against sporting estates.

On any one site it may be hard to decide whether overall the benefits for nature conservation that flow from the wood being managed for shooting (not least that the wood survives) outweigh the negative points. However most of the latter are in the control of the estate manager. He or she can reduce the impact of the more damaging aspects of sporting practice by, for example, putting release pens into new woodland or areas that have been replanted rather than into old semi-natural stands.

Pheasant shooting is the main sporting use of woods in much of the country. Other lowland field sports have less of an effect on woodland nature conservation. Locally badgers may be disturbed by fox hunting, but more significant is often the effect of large numbers of horses and hunt followers going through a wood during the hunt. This latter is similar to the effects of a sponsored charity ride, an orienteering event or some motor rallies and is considered below.

In the uplands sporting considerations have often been beneficial to wildlife, through providing a justification to increase the amount of open space within the forest. Ponds created for wildfowl and fishing, or lawns kept open to make it easier to shoot deer provide a welcome break among the dense stands of spruce or pine. The presence of black grouse or capercaillie provide additional arguments for retaining open heathy patches, scrub and overmature stands within commercial plantations, which might otherwise be lost.

Grouse shooting and deer stalking, which depend on open ground, are to some extent in competition with afforestation. Similarly salmon and trout fishing may be badly affected in some regions if too much of the catchment is planted up. Supporters of these sports at times make common cause with those wishing to protect the wildlife of the open moor from further afforestation.

The red deer population on the moors must however be brought under control in the interests of both forestry and nature conservation. A cull of 50,000 was proposed for 1990 by the Red Deer Commission to try to reduce the levels of overgrazing that prevent regeneration both in native pine and oakwoods and in commercial forests. Such a cull is long overdue and would reduce the numbers of deer that die each winter from bad weather and starvation. To be effective it depends on killing the does, not just the stags, which are more highly prized as trophies. It will also require considerable co-operation between adjacent estates if deer from one are not simply to walk across into the space created by shooting on the next. Some find it odd that nature conservation should be fostered by the killing of wild animals, but there are no longer the natural predators that would have killed deer in the past. If there are to be more natural woods there must be fewer deer in future.

A walk in the woods

One indirect consequence of intensive game management is that land owners become much more concerned about who goes into their woods; casual visitors are discouraged in case they disturb the game, let alone actually poach it. This and the strong feeling that the majority of the population who live in towns do not know how to behave considerately in the countryside (sometimes true) has meant that access to woodland has not been as free as it might have been. This is a pity because in many lowland counties woods are the most attractive places left in a landscape of otherwise intensive agriculture.

Surveys have shown that people do like to go to the countryside for a walk, even if on closer questioning this proves to be no more than 50 metres from their car. These folk regard woods as good places for picnic sites and for hiding the car parks, where they can sit and read the papers in peace. This is a fair enough attitude if picnic site and car park can be placed in areas where they cause no damage.

For the substantial minority who do go further there are many areas of open access woodland owned by local authorities, and charities such as the Woodland Trust and National Trust. As a rule the public can walk anywhere on Forestry Commission land, which includes over 10,000 miles of forestry tracks and 700 way-marked walks. In Grizedale Forest, Cumbria, there is even a 12-mile trail that includes sculptures made from wood, twigs and rocks. So far it has attracted over 200,000 visitors. Another has been set up in the Forest of Dean. Such enlightened attitudes to public access have not unfortunately always been carried over when Commission woods have been sold although recent legislation has sought to remedy this problem.

The majority of broadleaved woods are privately owned, but there are still rights of way by or through many of them. Some paths may be survivals from the time when local people needed to visit the woods to work or to collect their firewood. Now used mainly for pleasure, they are much more attractive than those that simply run through cornfields and ryegrass.

Even if the woods are private, the path and view from it are public. Strong passions may be roused by the sight of felled trees or even just the sound of a chainsaw near a favourite path, but it is better that people should care than that a wood should be lost or damaged through apathy or ignorance. Moves to protect local sites from road schemes or insensitive replanting can usually count on support from the dog-walkers and Sunday strollers' union.

Concern to maintain public open spaces fuelled the campaign to save Epping Forest in the nineteenth century; recently the same sorts of feeling led to opposition to the sale of popular woods owned by the water authorities when the latter were sold off as private companies. Local authorities can try to negotiate with owners to create new places for people to walk in woods, but this may prove expensive if the owner seeks compensation for loss of privacy.

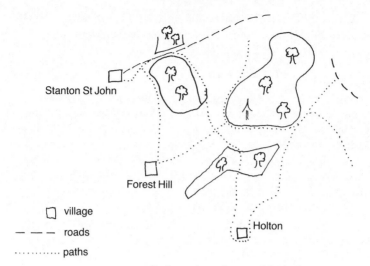

Stanton St John

Forest Hill

Holton

□ village
— — — roads
⋯⋯⋯⋯ paths

Paths and woods east of Oxford.

Some woodland walks exist where visitors pay for the privilege, often associated with spectacular riverside routes as used to be the case at Bolton Abbey or Thornton and Twistleton Glens near Skipton, but most are free. This makes it difficult to assess how much all these walks are worth to the community when compared to other uses of the wood or proposed developments, but this does not diminish their value.

Effects on the wood

Whatever the reason for entering a wood, most people stick to obvious paths except in very open or well used sites. Often they are concerned that they will get lost if they plough off into the undergrowth. Steep slopes, bracken, brambles and a dense understorey may make for difficult walking away from the path anyway, as woodland survey teams will confirm. Despite this, because trees and shrubs limit views, woods can often absorb many more people than for example open grassland without it seeming too crowded for the visitors. Damage or disturbance to wildlife may also be quite light over much of the site, but some problems do arise.

Forty years ago visitors to woods in spring were likely to come home with large bunches of flowers and perhaps a bird's egg or two. Collecting eggs is now illegal and people are encouraged to take home only pictures and memories of the blooms. The boots that trample the leaves are generally now more damaging than the hands that grasp the flowers. Around some popular beauty spots the vegetation is completely worn away and the soil so compacted that even tree roots suffer. Thus the Major oak at Sherwood had to be protected by a wooden fence to keep people away from it. Elsewhere paths spread as walkers avoid wet trampled patches or cut across corners. Horses and vehicles may make even quite wide rides a sticky morass in wet weather. This is undesirable since the grasses and flowers on the rides are destroyed, although the boggy patches and deep water-filled ruts may attract a few plant and animal species of their own!

There may be no alternative but to make up the paths with sand, gravel or wood chips, to cut steps and create special properly surfaced routes for riders. Part of the sense of wilderness is lost to ensure less damage to the wood overall; on a more positive note woods with such good paths are important so that the elderly, blind and disabled, the push-chairs and wheel-chairs are not excluded.

Organized activities

Woods are often used for organized sports and games from field archery to husky dog racing, simply because they contain the only open free space in much of the country. The Forestry Commission provides facilities for 64 motor rallies in its woods from international events to local club gatherings. One-off events, even if large numbers of people are involved, such as in a major orienteering championship, are unlikely to cause long-term disturbance to the wildlife, provided sensitive areas such as wetland and times such as the bird nesting season are avoided. It is much more difficult to accommodate regular use of woods by large numbers of people, not least because of the way that paths expand and increase and undergrowth is broken down.

Recently these problems have been brought to a head as woodland owners have tried to find alternative economic uses for their land. The explosive development of paint ball games, in which teams compete using guns that fire plastic pellets of paint, has caused particular concern. Sites have appeared all over the country, often in woods that are very important for nature conservation. The paint may be biodegradable but trees around campsites become heavily stained; litter may be left about; trampling damage can be very high and there is disturbance to the nesting bird-life in spring.

Woods are also becoming the favoured location for major leisure complexes with chalets or caravan parks and even complete domed-in holiday centres and dry ski-runs. The attraction for the developer of attractive surroundings is clear, but part of the wood is destroyed by the process and the rest is at risk of becoming little different from an urban park. Both the paint ball game expansion and other major proposals illustrate a common nature conservation problem; not how to stop developments, but how to restrict the damage to the least sensitive woodlands. Thus these activities should be steered away from the ancient semi-natural woods, to those new plantations where there is scope for creative conservation which will improve the wood for wildlife and for leisure use.

Seeing the woods or the trees

How does concern about the aesthetics of woodland affect wildlife? Often they go hand in hand: campaigns against large-scale afforestation and the conversion of broadleaved woods to conifers benefitted both. Landscape inspired changes such as felling large conifer forests in smaller blocks and allowing birch and willow to colonize streamsides help wildlife. Extracting timber carefully so as to avoid creating too much unsightly bare mud is less damaging to the ground flora. The regional variation that characterizes semi-natural woods and their wildlife provides much of the character of local landscapes; beech trees 'look right' in the Chilterns, just as pines do on Deeside.

Occasionally, though, views on landscape and nature conservation may conflict. One occasion was where the National Trust proposed in 1990 to fell 200 large Douglas fir at Skelwith Bridge in the Lake District, not far from the scene of some of the fiercest battles in the 1930s to prevent conifer afforestation. The Trust's aim was to plant oak and hazel to help restore part of an ancient wood to its former state – an admirable nature conservation aim. By this time, ironically local people regarded the firs as an attractive feature of the landscape, and wanted to keep them. Rhododendron in parts of North Wales contributes to the beauty of some scenic drives in spring, but in woods it is a pernicious weed that conservationists would like to eradicate. Then again, not everyone likes the look of a fresh cut coppice or the shape of pollards, although they may be superb for wildlife.

Woods are for people as well as for the primroses and pine trees. There are places and times when the needs of wildlife must come first, but in most cases woodland conservation can be combined with fun. In fact, perhaps fun is worth more than timber – but how do you measure these things? If people want old beeches and oaks rather than spruce, that may be good enough reason to keep woods as they are. Perhaps some timber production should be sacrificed to keep a particular view or for the anemones in spring. How, though, are such decisions to be reached and by whom? And who will pay the price for the lost income from the timber if losses there are?

IO

Now, if you would just
Fill in This Form . . .

The owners and managers of woods directly influence the wildlife they contain, but do not have a completely free hand in every case. This external control on what happens to woods is nothing new: the Bible contains strictures as to how trees are to be treated and by early medieval times common practice and laws governing woods and forests were well developed.

The forest in its medieval sense of an area to which special laws applied (mainly concerning deer) might be seen as something like the contemporary National Parks in England and Wales. National Parks are areas defined by the government, as the Forests were by the king, but where most of the land remains in private ownership. The land in modern Parks may include woodland but also farms and even villages and towns, as with the medieval Forest. Special 'rules', planning regulations and consultations on big planting schemes apply, the equivalent of the Forest laws that for example limited the fencing of woods in certain areas, prevented villagers from killing deer and punished them if they did. People in National Parks also regularly complain about the extra restrictions placed on them, just as our ancestors moaned about the Royal Forests.

Bureaucracy has been around for a very long while and the modern equivalent of the medieval Foresters is probably more likely to be found in local government rather than in the Forestry Commission! Modern foresters are the descendants of the woodmen and rangers charged with the protection and harvesting of the game and the wood or wood products from the Forest.

Modern controls and regulations

Controls on forests are far less stringent than those on land put to urban or industrial use, but increasingly the value of woods for the landscape and for wildlife should be considered alongside its value for the production of timber. An attractive landscape and abundant wildlife are benefits that society as a whole shares (or is deprived of if the wrong decisions are made) so that a wide range of voluntary and official bodies get involved in decisions to fell or plant trees. This may be resented, but town and country are not separate. People who live or work in towns depend on those in the country for their food, but country dwellers depend on towns and factories for fuel and markets for their products.

Who does what?

Central to discussions on forests and woodland, and hence effects on their wildlife, are the Forestry Commission. They themselves are one of the biggest land owners in the country and their forests are expected to be managed as models – with standards at least as high as those they impose on the private sector. Forestry Commission officers grant the licences needed before trees and woods can be felled and distribute grants to owners of private woods. They approve the plans that owners in receipt of such grants must submit every five years to say what felling or planting is planned. Every ten years or so a national census of woods and trees is organized; the last was from 1979-1982, and the next one will be beginning soon. But the Forestry Commission rarely are the only people involved.

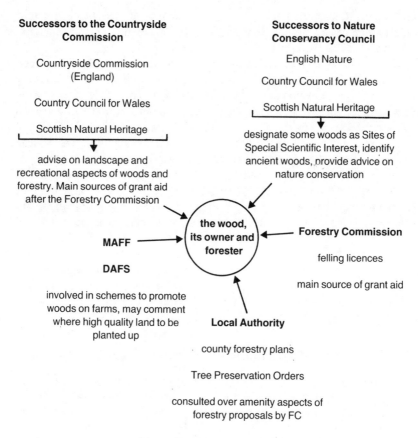

Main official bodies and their roles.

The Forestry Commission consults and seeks advice from a number of other bodies on a formal and informal basis. The district councils are usually asked for their views on the amenity aspects of planting or felling proposals which can be widely interpreted to mean either landscape or wildlife matters. District and County or Regional Councils also determine the fate of trees and woods affected by proposals that require planning permission such as house and road building schemes.

Where woods or open land are particularly important for nature conservation or in the landscape additional advice and comment would have been sought from the Nature Conservancy Council and the Countryside Commission – now reorganized into separate bodies for England, Wales and Scotland, who will take on this role – and voluntary conservation bodies such as the local wildlife trusts.

Where land is of particularly high farming value the agriculture departments may be asked to comment and there used to be an assumption that trees were not planted on good farming soils. This has changed somewhat in recent years as the need has arisen to take some land out of agricultural production to reduce European surpluses.

Not surprisingly it is not always possible to come up with a solution that pleases everyone. When agreement cannot be reached the case is considered by Regional Advisory Committees which comprise local respected foresters, owners or agents and representatives of other interests who try to find an acceptable compromise. Recent changes in procedures have made it easier for members of the public to put their views on a case: if the committee is meeting to discuss a particular proposal this will be advertised in the local paper and interested parties can send in their comments. If the committee fails to resolve the problems a scheme may have to go up to the Secretary of State to decide. Such cases are, fortunately, rare.

Consider the people involved in a case in 1984. A farmer applied to the Forestry Commission for permission to clear part of his wood to improve the profitability of his farm; Ministry of Agriculture officials confirmed that this was necessary to maintain the income of the farmer. On the other hand local people were concerned that the footpath through the wood would no longer be such an attractive walk; the Nature Conservancy Council believed that clearance should not be permitted because too much valuable ancient woodland had already been lost in this way; another swathe of bluebells would go under the plough. In this instance the decision reached was that the wood should not be cleared.

Ironically a neighbouring wood had been felled illegally a few years previously. Sometimes through ignorance, rarely with malice aforethought, owners go in with the chainsaw or bulldozer without getting permission first. The first line of protection for the wood and its wildlife is then usually the Tree Preservation Order. These are the responsibility of the local district council and may be applied either to individual trees or to blocks of woodland. Anyone who believes that a wood or a tree is of high amenity value and is under threat in some way or other should apply to their district council to have such an order made. Once the order is made, the owner must apply to the council before the tree can be cut down so that the case for keeping it can be reviewed. A recent proposal means that it may be possible in future to protect hedges in a similar way.

The first ports of call for an outsider interested in a woodland or forestry case are therefore the officer in the local district council responsible for trees and woodland (generally in the planning or parks department) and the local Forestry Commission office. The latter is also the commonest source of advice and assistance for the woodland owner.

And who pays?

The problem with forestry, particularly new planting on bare ground, is that money has to be invested to buy the land and to plant the trees, but the returns from felling them may be anything from thirty to a hundred years away. There are arguments within the forestry world, between foresters and the Treasury, and between foresters and others concerned with land use about just how profitable (if at all) forestry is in such circumstances. Might the money be better placed elsewhere, including in forestry projects in the Tropics, for example? So far the government has always ended up deciding that supporting both state and private forests is worthwhile, although the means and the conditions attached have varied over the years.

The Forestry Commission

The Forestry Commission itself, when it was set up in 1919, had to make substantial investments to buy and plant land to expand the area of state-owned forests. There was little in the way of return from these forests for a long time, while the trees were growing. Many of those early forests are old enough now to be harvested so returns are coming from timber sales, from other activities on Commission land (such as camping sites) and from the sales of whole blocks of forest land to private investors in line with the government's policy during the '80s. These offset some of the costs of running the organization and planting new ground. Many of the forests created since 1945 have still to reach their first harvest, so the Commission has not yet broken even on its annual accounts, although it expects to do so shortly.

In 1939 the Forestry Commission's new forests were too young to contribute much to the timber demands of the Second World War and as a consequence about half the timber standing in private forests had to be felled. Controls on felling were introduced to ensure regular supply of material to the mills. Afterwards it was decided that private owners needed to be encouraged to restock the woods that had been cleared. New grant schemes were introduced for this purpose. The details of these have changed over the years. On the one hand there has been pressure to make the system simpler, by limiting consultation and cutting out annual management payments; on the other there have been demands that the grants should reflect the changing expectations of what the public wants from forests, since public money is being used.

Owners have been encouraged since the mid '70s to discuss with local authorities the possibilities of public access to their woods. Higher grant rates were introduced for broadleaved trees and for Scots pine to encourage the use of native trees which will generally produce woods richer in wildlife and a more attractive landscape than the standard spruces or larch. Recently these higher rates of grant for more 'environmentally friendly' forestry have been backed up by management guidelines. While owners are not bound by such guidelines there is strong pressure to follow them.

Forestry was also supported through special tax arrangements whereby the costs of planting could be offset against income earned in other ways – from being a pop star, a local businessman or from other activities on the estate such as operating a sawmill or farming. Tax incentives became controversial partly because many (including treasury officials) believed that if such forestry support was justified it should be done openly through increased grants and not hidden in the tax system. Tax incentives were also associated with the funding of some of the most damaging afforestation schemes of the late '70s and early '80s: the planting that led to the destruction of large areas of natural peat bogs in Caithness and Sutherland. Some even questioned whether such plantings would ever produce a worthwhile timber crop and quite suddenly the tax rules were changed in the budget of 1988. The rate of new planting in the northern peatlands dropped dramatically.

The tax relief system did have some benefits for nature conservation. It was used by estates in the lowlands as a means of funding management work in woods during the early part of the rotation when there was little income from the trees. The need to support such activities led to renewed calls for some form of a management grant for work that is done primarily for environmental benefit. Such a grant became available from April 1992.

There is still an expectation in woods where work is funded by the Forestry Commission that some timber will be produced. This was and still can be a drawback since there are conflicts between wood production and wildlife. Some types of management, for example coppicing, have been difficult, usually impossible to fit into the forestry grant system (although it should fall within the scope of the new management grants). Other proposals did not have much timber production potential, particularly small-scale plantings and so simply did not qualify for forestry grants.

There are various other sources of funds: the Countryside Commission for England and Wales was probably the biggest source of grant for amenity woodland schemes, usually working through the county councils. Millions of trees have been put in with this support, in field corners, along hedgerows to replace elms and in woodlands. Many of these trees have died subsequently through lack of aftercare. It might be better if the emphasis was less on planting and more on looking after the trees and woodland we already have and on protecting self-sown seedlings. Nevertheless the countryside would be more bleak in many areas without such efforts.

Trees and woods on working farms can be funded through various schemes from the departments of agriculture. There are schemes for planting new hedges (that for grubbing out hedges has thankfully been abandoned) and for planting new shelterbelts and there is now a special farm woodland scheme designed to help reduce the European Community surpluses of grain and livestock. In the uplands other grants may be used to fence woods to improve their conservation value by allowing regeneration to occur.

Used imaginatively and sympathetically, the variety of different sources of money can do much for nature conservation, but there is also always the risk that trees will be planted in the wrong place (on flower-rich meadows for example). One of the roles of the Nature Conservancy Council, as it was for its forerunner and is for its successors, was to make sure that this does not happen.

What about nature conservation?

In 1949 the government set up the Nature Conservancy to look after wildlife, first of all by creating nature reserves. Secondly it was to identify other important areas and advise their owners and local authorities about their value so that they might not be damaged inadvertently. To do this a large number of surveys and research projects on the best forms of management for these sites were needed. These tasks have been carried on after 1973 by the Nature Conservancy Council, and from 1.4.1991 by its successors, the Scottish Natural Heritage Agency, the Countryside Council for Wales and English Nature, following the latest reorganization.

Continuing to make an invaluable contribution throughout this period have been the voluntary conservation societies. These have helped with surveys and site management and by alerting people to the losses of wildlife that were taking place. They also own many important woods, for example Hatfield Forest in Essex (National Trust), Ebernoe Common (Sussex Wildlife Trust), Hoddesdon Park Wood in Hertfordshire (Woodland Trust) and Abernethy Forest (Speyside) (RSPB).

A major concern of the Nature Conservancy Council was to protect the cream of British woodland and other habitats, such as the best moorland areas, for their wildlife. These precious places are lumbered with the unglamorous name of Sites of Special Scientific Interest. The woods so chosen are spread across the country to include as much as possible of the variation that has been described earlier. The majority are ancient semi-natural woods because these are the richest and the most natural. Even so, only about a fifth of this category, less than ten per cent of all British woods, can be included.

Some sites are large and well known, including the New Forest and most of the native pinewoods of Scotland. Others are small and their special value may be obvious only to a specialist. Some in North Wales are picked for their mosses; woods in Kent provide outstanding examples of hornbeam-wood anemone communities; in a wood in northern England lurks the last wild Lady's Slipper Orchid while a birchwood in Sutherland sits perched on blocks of rock the size of houses.

Most of these woods are privately owned, so the Nature Conservancy Council has had to try to make sure that the owners, the Forestry Commission and district councils are aware of their importance. These functions have been passed on to the three new agencies – Countryside Council for Wales, Scottish Natural Heritage Agency and English Nature. Then there should be little excuse for unintentional damage to woodland SSSIs. It is also necessary to look at how they are being treated at present and whether this needs to be altered in future. A fence might be needed to stop heavy grazing by sheep; some coppicing might be desirable to create the open sunny glades that butterflies need; while in a few the best thing for the wildlife there at present is to do nothing at all.

If the owner wishes to change the way he/she manages a wood, the relevant statutory nature conservation agency has to be consulted first so that damaging changes can be limited. If what is best for nature conservation would lead to an owner being out of pocket, then compensation may be paid and some sort of management agreement prepared.

At times this process is quite effective but at others it is cumbersome and does not give particularly good value for money. Compensation claims can be for thousands of pounds per year on some sites. Also the system works mainly by preventing people from doing things rather than by encouraging positive work and a pride in the wildlife on the site.

In particularly sensitive sites it may be better if the wood is bought by a conservation organization which can then run it as a reserve. There are 87 woods owned or managed as National Nature Reserves run by the three nature conservation agencies in addition to the many owned by the RSPB, the County Wildlife Trusts, the National Trust and the Woodland Trust. Frequently local members of these voluntary conservation societies play a major role in the management of the reserves, as well as in the recording of the plants and animals they contain.

What a mess . . .

This welter of grants, rules, designations and organizations has been the despair of many a woodland owner and many a conservationist. It is easy to suggest that it could and should be made simpler, but perhaps there are some advantages in its diversity. The different organizations provide a check on each other, the various grants appeal to different types of people and a voluntary conservation organization can often move to save a wood a lot more quickly than the ponderous tread of government bodies. Time and again it is the voice of the local people and groups that tips the balance in deciding what ought to happen.

One way to simplify matters is through one-stop agencies and projects such as Coed Cymru. Coed Cymru means Welsh Wood and it is an imaginative scheme funded by the various bodies concerned with the countryside in Wales. Its officers provide advice to farmers in particular, as to how to get the most from their woods to meet a whole range of objectives. It has been so successful with more that a thousand small schemes now under its belt that the problem is keeping up with the interest that is generated.

Coed Cymru is just one of a number of such local schemes that have appeared in recent years. There is one called Sylvanus in the West Country, another long-running scheme in Sussex, called ESUS, while Scottish Community Woodlands operates north of the Border. Each is organized in a slightly different way, enabling it to reflect local needs and build on local strengths.

There are other ways in which people are trying to work together for conservation. A large block of woodland in Kent was recently bought by a consortium consisting of Kent County Council, Swale Borough Council, Canterbury City Council, the RSPB, the Woodland Trust and a private owner (with some funds from the Nature Conservancy Council). This woodland in the Blean is a stronghold of the heath fritillary and has one per cent of the nightingale population in Britain. The land purchased links up three existing reserves to form one of the largest protected broadleaved woods in the lowlands. The purchase would have been beyond the reach of any one of the consortium members on their own.

We do however live in a country where land is limited. If resources are put into saving one wood they will not be available to save the next that comes under threat. Thus there must be some view as to what the priorities for woodland conservation should be; what is the minimum we should aim for in terms of sites protected and what happens to them. We must then strive to make sure that what we achieve goes beyond that minimum. Most of all we need a vision as to what sort of woodland we want to have.

I I

Woodland Conservation: Now and in the Future

There are likely to be more woods in Britain in the year 2000 than there are now, but will this be judged to be good or bad for nature conservation? Will populations of rare woodland plants and animals have been maintained or will some have become extinct? Will woods in general be richer in wildlife than they are now or will most appear dull and uninteresting? Most important of all, will our stock of semi-natural woodland have been kept and expanded or will yet more woods have been turned into monotonous plantations unrelated to regional and local history and environment?

Woodland nature conservation will have failed if the rate of conversion of ancient semi-natural woods to plantations is not greatly reduced and if rich upland moors continue to be planted. Foresters' zeal to increase the woodland area everywhere and to increase wood production on existing sites must be tempered if the mistakes of the past fifty years are not to be repeated.

Fortunately new woods and forests created in the next ten years are likely to be richer than those planted in the past because of improvements in forest design. New guidelines specify that a minimum of 5 per cent of the ground in new upland plantations is to be planted with broadleaved trees as a rule. Planting is to be kept back from streamsides. There is also beginning to be a consensus on the need to shift new afforestation away from valuable moorland, rich grassland and irreplaceable bogs. More is being done to alter forest management in existing woods so that long-established plant and animal communities can survive under modern regimes. Regional guidelines are being produced to complement national advice.

In many upland woods there is overgrazing by sheep and deer, which prevents woodland regeneration almost totally. Such grazing needs to be controlled, if we are not to lose these woods by default. Some recreational uses of woods may have to be stopped if we are not to destroy that which we have come to value and enjoy. Roads, quarries and housing developments must be prevented from nibbling away at woods. The opportunities for creative conservation in connection with urban and community forests must be seen and grasped.

Those whose primary interests are wildlife need to review what it is reasonable to try to achieve. We must look beyond the barricades of Sites of Special Scientific Interest and National Nature Reserves; beyond assumptions that things must be kept exactly as they are, that traditional management is the answer to everything. There are ways of using modern methods to achieve the continuity of habitat conditions formerly provided by, for example, coppice regimes. Change may be unavoidable in some woods; it may be natural in some woods while in others it may need to be controlled within specified limits.

New challenges are constantly arising. Several surveys have shown that the health of beech trees is declining. Is this an effect of air pollution, in which case the decline may well continue unless controls on emissions from power stations and the like are tightened, or are the effects seen just the consequences of old age and drought? It is argued both ways, but prudence would point to us controlling pollution. Is the spate of recent oak deaths just due to weather or has a new disease appeared? There is no clear answer yet, but the consequences of Dutch Elm Disease on the landscape are an unwelcome precedent. Should we be doing more to establish links between woods so that, if global warming alters our climate, the chances for species to migrate from one to another are increased?

Everywhere the understanding and goodwill of woodland owners and managers will be essential if there is not to be further loss of species through neglect, or through adherence to the letter, rather than the spirit of conservation policies.

Woodland priorities

The different types of wood discussed in this book all contribute something to the overall aims of woodland conservation. There are however immense differences in their potential for improvement and in the losses for wildlife that will occur if they are mismanaged. Awareness of this must guide priorities in both policy and practice. For example, Kielder Forest plantations are unlikely ever to have the same overall value as the ancient woods in Borrowdale, however much money is poured into creating broadleaved corridors and altering the size of the areas felled.

Two hundred years would be needed to create afresh oakwoods such as those planted after the Napoleonic wars; and it is doubtful if we can ever reasonably expect to duplicate the conditions in semi-natural woods that have existed since the medieval period. Therefore protecting the best of what we have and that which it is most difficult to replace is a good starting point.

This is also likely to be the cheapest option where, as it usually does, nature conservation requires some reduction in timber or agricultural production. Less land is needed to achieve the same wildlife benefit if resources are put into protection of the richest areas. At the same time increasing our stock of highly productive plantations on land of little intrinsic wildlife value – arable or improved grassland in particular – will enable us to make a contribution to reducing international forest degradation with the minimum disadvantages for nature conservation in Britain.

The first priority must be to protect and improve the management of ancient semi-natural woods. These are only about 15 per cent of the total woodland, and they require the most sensitive treatment. Any changes that we make in them should be done with caution although at times we get alarmed about short-term changes because they are unfamiliar, forgetting perhaps that even greater changes occurred in the past. The broad principles of what is needed are easily stated:

- Maintain the trees and shrubs native to particular sites so that the distinctive character of Britain's ancient woods is maintained and so too are the important regional differences that separate the woods of Kent and Caithness, Norfolk and North Wales.
- Promote variety in the structure of stands and woods to produce the different conditions on which the diversity of woodland species depends. How that is done can vary from wood to wood and from county to county: in the south-east the emphasis may be on restoring coppice systems; in the west on controlling grazing in upland oakwoods; in high forests on keeping any felling small-scale and encouraging old trees.
- Avoid standard prescriptions; rather capitalize on the features that are special to a particular wood. Thus in wood pastures, look to maintain the mixture of open woodland with large veteran trees and open grown pollards; in worked coppice woods concentrate on keeping a regular amount of open ground and glades; in pinewoods keep the mixture of old trees, open bogs and locally dense regeneration zones.
- Let some woods and some parts of woods run wild; interfere as little as possible and just see what happens when nature is allowed to largely take its own course.
- Be aware of the possibilities and pitfalls of the various ways in which ancient woods have come to be used, of the effects of grazing or game rearing, of paint ball games and horse riding. They can more than pay for the maintenance of the wood in some circumstances, but can wreck it in others just as easily as intensive timber production.

In the south and east another priority is to try to restore plantations on ancient sites to some semblance of their former glory, as has been demonstrated by the Forestry Commission and others at sites such as Tyddesley Wood and Chalkney Wood. Remove introduced trees and shrubs; encourage any surviving native species and re-introduce them as necessary. Get as much light and life down to the forest floor as possible by heavy thinning and ride widening.

A concerted programme of ancient woodland restoration would help compensate for the thousands of hectares of ancient woodland grubbed out for fields and factories over the last fifty years which can never be recovered. Even so ancient woods will remain as mainly small and isolated units vulnerable to changes around them. Such vulnerability can be reduced by allowing them to expand on to adjacent land and encouraging new woodland to form connecting corridors and stepping stones to help species spread. That this is a realistic possibility is suggested by the way that recent woods in the uplands and areas like the Weald that have always been well wooded are already generally richer than more isolated new woods. Such links may become even more important if our climate changes, forcing species to migrate or become extinct on the sites where they now occur.

There are areas where it might be possible to recreate the original tree line by protection from grazing. Over time the thin scattered remnants of trees along streams might spread across adjacent slopes. No timber could be produced from such high altitude woods, but we might find some surprises in how our open moorland species cope with a restoration of the former vegetation cover of the hills.

Meanwhile what should be happening with new plantations on open ground that already exist? To some extent they can be used judiciously with new semi-natural woods to reduce the isolation of ancient woods, particularly where native trees can be used, or if not at least species with similar characteristics to our native trees. Within them pockets of variation, glades, patches of native species, streamsides, old open stands can be protected and woven into a conservation network.

Recent woods and plantations can also be used for those activities that need a woodland setting but would be particularly damaging in ancient semi-natural woods. These range from intensive timber production to war games. Thus the pressure can be taken off the best sites in another way.

A pipe dream?

Can the above be achieved? Woodland is marked on existing maps and the location of most ancient woods is now known through the work of the Nature Conservancy Council who have prepared lists of them on a county or district basis. Several counties in England and Wales and some Scottish regions are considering or have prepared forestry and woodland strategies. These can serve as a catalyst for bringing together the main groups of people involved with woods in an area and highlighting the broad areas of accord and discord between woodland uses. Even where such formal mechanisms do not exist the key individuals involved probably already know one another, so informal local groupings can work.

The grants available to owners not just for forestry in the accepted sense but for countryside management generally are becoming more flexible and imaginative. Conservation bodies are becoming stronger in the sense that they are more able to buy key areas and then to manage them, but are also appreciating that often there may be a wood product at the end. New uses and users of the wood are needed. Traditional crafts can play a part but there are large amounts of produce to be shifted if ancient semi-natural woods are not always to be a drain on the public's or the owner's purse.

Forestry needs clear long-term goals and preferably ones that do not change too much during the life of a tree. We encourage governments in tropical countries to have a plan for the protection and exploitation of their forests, but we do not seem to have one ourselves. At best we have annual planting targets set by the government which have seldom been met in recent years. Such open-ended commitments are not very helpful because there must be some point beyond which any government would regard further expansion to be undesirable, but this is not stated. Also the forestry industry rightly points out that such targets have little meaning if other government policies and commitments, including those to do with nature conservation, prevent them reaching the desired level of planting. A target of 1.5–2 million hectares of productive forest was set in 1919 and reiterated in 1943 but this has now been met. Where should forestry go from here?

There are those who argue for forestry to be brought under planning control, for large new afforestation schemes in particular to be subject to the same scrutiny as a factory or housing development. There are moves taking place in this direction. Planning control however is simply another mechanism for trying to achieve a fair balance of objectives. It may not be any better than the mechanisms that already exist *if* people can be persuaded to use them constructively.

The role of the individual in achieving woodland conservation is crucial. There are very few owners and woodland managers who are not interested in nature conservation; some may not appreciate the importance of their particular wood; others do, but cannot see how they can maintain its interest, given the various constraints that may be placed on them. Such people need help and encouragement. Whether or not you own a wood you can help by finding out about those in your area, which ones are ancient, how they have been treated in the past, what threats they are under, what role they have in the local community. You can try to influence the views of local authorities to encourage them to use their powers to promote woodland conservation. You can perhaps help with the management of a local reserve, encourage your parish council to take an interest in its trees and woods, be a tree warden or simply join one of the voluntary organizations that look after woods and their wildlife.

This book may have taught you something about Britain's woods in a general sense, but it cannot tell you anything about the wood just down the road. You must go there and look for yourself, whether it is a clump of sycamores on the old railway track or a medieval ash-maple coppice on the parish boundary. Try to see it in its context, how it has developed, how it may change. It may be rich or poor in wildlife (part of the fun is trying to work out why it is as it is) but it has a part to play in making sure that the next decade is rather better than the previous half-century for woodland conservation.

There will always be some tension between the commercial forester and the conservationist so I do not expect the hatchet to be buried. I do hope however that it will be more often applied to the right tree.

Further Reading

Anderson, M.L., *A History of Scottish Forestry* (Nelson, London, 1967)

Avery, M., & R. Leslie, *Birds and Forestry* (Poyser, London, 1990)

Fry, R., & D. Lonsdale, *Habitat Management For Insects* (Amateur Entomologists Society Handbook 21, 1991)

Gray, N., *Woodland Management for Pheasants and Wildlife* (David & Charles, Newton Abbot, 1986)

Harris, J.G.S., *Trees and the Law* (Agricultural Association, Romsey)

Hibberd, B.G., *Forestry Practice*, Forestry Commission Handbook 6 (HMSO, London, 1991)

Linnard, W., *Welsh Woods and Forests* (National Museum of Wales, Cardiff, 1982)

Marren, P., *The Wildwoods* (David & Charles, Newton Abbot, 1992)

Marren, P., *Woodland Heritage* (David & Charles, Newton Abbot, 1990)

Peterken, G.F., *Woodland Conservation and Management* (Chapman & Hall, London, 1981)

Rackham, O., *History of the Countryside* (Dent, London, 1986)

Rackham, O., *Trees and Woodland in the British Landscape*, 2nd ed. (Dent, London, 1990)

Sinden, N., *In a Nut-shell* (Common Ground, London, 1989)

Smart, N., & J. Andrews, *Birds and Broadleaves* (RSPB, Sandy, 1985)

Tompkins, S., *Forestry in Crisis* (Helm, Bromley, 1989)

Watkins, C., *Woodland Management and Conservation* (David & Charles, Newton Abbot, 1990)

Useful addresses

Countryside Council for Wales*
Plas Penrhos
Ffordd Penrhos
Bangor
Gwynedd LL57 2LQ

National Trust
36 Queen Anne's Gate
London SW1H 9AS

National Trust for Scotland
5 Charlotte Square
Edinburgh EH2 4DU

English Nature (Nature Conservancy for England) *
Northminster House
Peterborough
PE1 1UA

Royal Society for the Protection of Birds
The Lodge
Sandy
Beds SG19 2DL

Scottish National Heritage
12 Hope Terrace
Edinburgh EH9 2AS

Forestry Commission*
231 Corstorphine Road
Edinburgh
EH12 7AT

Countryside Commission for England
John Dower House
Crescent Place
Cheltenham
Glos GL50 3RA

Royal Society for Nature
    Conservation
(the umbrella body for the various
    local wildlife trusts†)
Witham Park
Lincoln LN5 7JR

Woodland Trust
Autumn Park
Dysart Rd
Grantham
Lincs
NG31 6LL

* these are the headquarters but there are also regional offices whose addresses can be found in the local telephone directory.

† the address of your local Trust will be in the telephone directory or can be obtained from the Royal Society for Nature Conservation.

Index